HOW TO SUCCEED
IN YOUR HOME BUSINESS
Second Edition

Larry Easto

DOUBLEDAY
TORONTO   NEW YORK   LONDON   SYDNEY   AUCKLAND

Canadian Cataloguing in Publication Data
Easto, Larry, 1944–
    How to succeed in your home business
    Rev. ed.
Includes bibliographical references and index.
ISBN 0–385–25516-0
1. Home-based businesses. I. Title.
HD2333.E27 1995   658'.041   C95–930715–X

Cover design and illustration by Greg Salmela
Text design by Heidy Lawrance Associates
Printed and bound in the USA

Published in Canada by
Doubleday Canada Limited
105 Bond Street
Toronto, Ontario
M5B 1Y3

To my mother, who passed away suddenly, just before this edition was conceived; we miss her — life goes on.

To my father, who continues to demonstrate that common sense and integrity are keys to success. Thanks, Dad.

To my wife, who kept the faith and provided unshakable support — for two editions. Thank you, Connie. I love you.

CONTENTS

ACKNOWLEDGMENTS

Many of us who operate home businesses spend a large number of hours alone. Few of us succeed in any project without the help of others.

This is particularly true of this book. Thousands of people purchased the first edition—self published by a first-time author. In doing so, they demonstrated that there is a place for a work like this. I appreciate their very tangible support. Hundreds of home business people have told me about their hopes and dreams, their concerns and fears. To these people I say: keep up the great work; may you continue to be an inspiration to others.

Many individuals played a role in bringing this book about. Norm Lingard, of the city of Brampton Small Business Self Help Office, arranged two sold-out workshops to help promote the first edition and continues to provide good advice and reliable information. Greg Salmela dipped into his limitless supply of creativity to design and illustrate another eye-catching cover. My editor (no name necessary) polished and tightened the manuscript. Thank you all for your talents and your help.

The people at Doubleday Canada deserve special thanks. They have consistently demonstrated that a publisher–author relationship need not be adversarial. Thanks to Gloria Goodman, Maggie Reeves and Christine Innes. It is great working with you.

PREFACE
TO THE
SECOND EDITION

I began working on the first edition of this book in the fall of 1992. Since that time I have spoken to hundreds of people who either operate a business from home or are thinking of doing so. During that period, I have witnessed a number of exciting developments that affect home businesses. I have also come to appreciate why, although alternatives are often available, individuals choose to continue to operate their businesses from home.

The most significant development has been the increased respectability of home businesses. Until fairly recently, few people were willing to talk openly about their businesses being home-based. There was a perception that home businesses were not "real businesses." Instead, they were thought to be temporary or part-time jobs or "hobby-businesses." Once those people operating businesses from their homes got "real jobs" (i.e., full-time paid employment away from the home), they would abandon their "hobbies" and everything would return to normal. Alternatively, if they were really serious about their businesses, once they made enough money they would move their businesses from their homes and operate like "real businesses."

Over the past few years, we have come to acknowledge home businesses as "real." Recent estimates suggest that there are approximately 45 million such businesses in the USA and Canada. These businesses spend more than $425 billion on goods and services annually. A market segment of this magnitude must be taken seriously. Not surprisingly, suppliers of everything from accounting services to work stations are now aggressively marketing to home businesses.

As well as the growth in numbers, the increased diversity of home business activities has become quite remarkable. Once the exclusive domain of craftspeople and individuals providing personal services, the home business sector now includes a wide spectrum of business activities ranging from high-level consulting to manufacturing, from leasing heavy equipment to writing.

Decentralization, driven in large part by innovations in computer technology and telecommunication services, has helped us realize that many business functions can be performed away from large centralized facilities. We have also learned that many business functions can be performed more effectively and efficiently by contracting them out to independent third parties.

Working in tandem, these two trends — decentralization and contracting out — have facilitated the development of a vast array of services offered by and available to home businesses. Small manufacturers can, for example, contract out the production and physical distribution of their products and perform functions such as design, marketing and general management from their home offices. Similarly, lessors of heavy equipment can manage their businesses from home while their inventory is stored elsewhere.

Using our personal computers and modems at home,

we have easy access to a variety of computer networks. This means that we no longer have to leave our homes and to go to traditional offices to use computer terminals linked to large mainframes. We can research our writing projects by accessing information data bases via the Internet, instead of working our way through printed library materials. It is no longer necessary to perform all business functions at centralized locations; many of these tasks, in fact, may be performed more effectively and efficiently from home offices.

While witnessing the growth of all forms of small businesses, including home businesses, we have also seen the breakdown of regional and national markets and the increased development of a global marketplace. How do we reconcile these two seemingly contradictory trends? John Naisbitt, author of several best-selling books, including *Megatrends* and *Megatrends 2000*, has noticed these same two developments and described them as a global paradox: ". . . the bigger the world economy, the more powerful its smaller players."[1] Naisbitt tells us that smaller players can align themselves in networks of entrepreneurs and in strategic alliances and play important roles in our new global economy. Thus, notwithstanding the increasing size of our marketplace, home businesses will continue to be important components of the global economy.

External factors such as the economy aside, those of us who choose to operate our businesses from home do so for one very important but nonetheless simple reason: we like it. We like the freedom, the independence and the job satisfaction that are the fringe benefits of our businesses. Freedom for us could be the freedom to wear casual, comfortable clothing or freedom from commuter travel. Independence means working on projects we like with people we enjoy. Job satisfaction for me includes working in a big, bright office with patio doors looking out on a well-used bird feeder. Like millions of others, I like what I am doing and love where I am doing it.

I am often asked whether home businesses are a short-term phenomenon, likely to fade as quickly as they appear to have developed or whether they are likely to remain economically viable over the long term. Responding to the question, I try to refer to the points outlined above. My questioners are often surprised when they find themselves agreeing that home businesses will continue to thrive in our quickly changing world.

Home businesses can and do provide a wide variety of goods and services profitably and enjoyably. For a growing number of people, they have come to represent the ideal business format.

Larry Easto

INTRODUCTION
How Entrepreneurial are you?

Operating any business from home requires more than having a quality product or service. Possessing a broad range of entrepreneurial skills and attitudes is just as important.

The following assessment will provide some insight as to your entrepreneurial orientation. Psychologists, successful entrepreneurs and consultants believe these attitudes and behavioral patterns are related to your ultimate success as an entrepreneur. Scoring instructions and suggestions as to possible interpretations follow the assessment.

As with any self-assessment, your final score and rating are not as important as the consideration that you give to the issues raised as you complete the exercise. You may be required to think about questions and concepts that are new to you. If this happens, address the issue as thoroughly as you can. Entrepreneurs, especially those operating home businesses, do not always have the luxury of ducking issues by referring them to someone else for resolution.

PART I: ATTITUDES TOWARD RISK TAKING

	Definitely Yes	Probably Yes	Probably No	Definitely No
1. I am prepared to make sacrifices in my family life and to take a cut in pay to succeed in my own business.	☐	☐	☐	☐
2. I take risks for the thrill of it.	☐	☐	☐	☐
3. I enjoy doing something just to prove that I can.	☐	☐	☐	☐
4. I enjoy tackling a task even without knowing all the potential problems.	☐	☐	☐	☐

PART II: PERSONAL INITIATIVE AND DISCIPLINE

	Definitely Yes	Probably Yes	Probably No	Definitely No
5. Once I decide to do something, I will do it and nothing can stop me.	☐	☐	☐	☐
6. When I begin a task, I set clear goals and objectives for myself.	☐	☐	☐	☐
7. After a severe setback in a project, I am able to pick up the pieces and start over again.	☐	☐	☐	☐

8. I am usually able to come up with more than one way to solve a problem.

☐ ☐ ☐ ☐

9. I believe in organizing my tasks before getting started.

☐ ☐ ☐ ☐

10. I find myself constantly thinking up new ideas.

☐ ☐ ☐ ☐

11. I can concentrate on one subject for extended periods of time.

☐ ☐ ☐ ☐

12. I find unexpected energy resources as I tackle things I like.

☐ ☐ ☐ ☐

13. I am likely to work long hours to accomplish a goal.

☐ ☐ ☐ ☐

PART III: GENERAL ATTITUDES

	Definitely Yes	Probably Yes	Probably No	Definitely No
14. When I do a good job, I am satisfied in knowing that the job has been well done.	☐	☐	☐	☐

15. I like the feeling of being in charge. ☐ ☐ ☐ ☐

16. When I think of the future, I envision myself running my own business. ☐ ☐ ☐ ☐

17. I try to do a better job than is expected of me. ☐ ☐ ☐ ☐

18. Personal satisfaction means more to me than having money to spend on myself. ☐ ☐ ☐ ☐

19. I try to find the benefits in a bad situation. ☐ ☐ ☐ ☐

20. I persist when others tell me it can't be done. ☐ ☐ ☐ ☐

21. I enjoy being able to make my own decisions on the job. ☐ ☐ ☐ ☐

22. I can accept failure without admitting defeat. ☐ ☐ ☐ ☐

23. I strive to use past mistakes as learning processes. ☐ ☐ ☐ ☐

24. I find that answers to problems come out of nowhere. ☐ ☐ ☐ ☐

25. I prefer to make final decisions on my own. ☐ ☐ ☐ ☐

SCORING:

The above questions all reflect traditional entrepreneurial attitudes. Scoring for these questions is:

4 points for each question answered "Definitely yes".
3 points for each question answered "Probably yes".
2 points for each question answered "Probably no".
1 point for each question answered "Definitely no".

INTERPRETATION:

Total Score

above 75   **Definitely Entrepreneurial**
Your combination of personal background and behavior and lifestyle patterns should give you the basis for a successful business.

50 – 74   **Possibly Entrepreneurial**
You might have the basis for a successful business. The assessments involved in preparing your business plan can serve as a second opinion as to whether you should proceed with the development of your own business.

26 – 49   **Probably Not Entrepreneurial**
Other possibilities may be more suitable to your personality and attitudes. There are many resources such as *What Color Is Your Parachute?* listed in Chapter 18.

under 25   **Definitely Not Entrepreneurial**
This is self-explanatory; you will probably work best as an employee.

It is prudent to bear in mind that many people, because of their temperament, attitudes, life circumstances and past experiences are more likely to be happy and productive as employees than as entrepreneurs.

PART
I

HOME
BUSINESS
AND YOU

1

THE GROWTH OF HOME BUSINESS

Our society is changing more dramatically and more rapidly than at any other time in history. At one time it was thought that the harder you worked, the better off you would be. We now know that hard work does not always lead to personal and economic success. Nor is it always good for the body: the stress-related consequences of working too hard are well known.

Millions of people are learning that bigger is not necessarily better. Mass layoffs at seemingly invincible giants like General Motors suggest that long-term security in large organizations is more myth than reality. Cutbacks and contracting out services have resulted in the loss of millions of jobs in North America.

Fortunately, there is light on the economic horizon. Home businesses will continue to thrive in an increasingly competitive marketplace.

Millions of entrepreneurs already enjoy running their own businesses from home. Over the next few years, millions more will join their ranks. There are many reasons for this growth.

Here are some of them.

BEATING STRESS

Individually and collectively, we know more about stress and stress management than any other generation in history. Hardly a week goes by without some authority telling us that we should watch our diets, exercise more, smoke and drink less — ideally, not at all — and generally improve the ways in which we manage our work and home lives. We are exposed to enough information on the subject that we should all be experts on the subject of "burnout."

Although acutely aware of the negative impact of too much work, many individuals are driven by the desire for more money or more status. They work more rather than fewer hours. Like shooting stars, they are on the rise; like shooting stars, they will sooner or later burn themselves out.

Fortunately, an increasing number of people are accepting the validity of various stress warnings and are committed to beating burnout. For many of these individuals, operating businesses from their homes helps to eliminate a large volume of work-related stress.

Obviously, commuting and its broad range of associated hassles becomes a non-issue when running a business from home. Best of all, the hours that would otherwise have been spent commuting can be put to better use.

People whose jobs involve working on computers and talking on telephones find their time more productive and less stressful when performed in the agreeable environment of a home office. At a time when many people merely *talk* about changing their lifestyles to improve the quality of their lives, those who work at home are actually *doing* it. The shift from busy, climate-controlled office premises to a more relaxed home environment eliminates most of the

workaday stressors: noise, crowding and unwelcome interruptions. With less time required for commuting, there is
more time for family and personal interests. This affords the
individual a more balanced lifestyle. The desire to minimize
stress and improve one's quality of life will continue to
encourage the trend to home businesses.

BREAKING BARRIERS

Pay equity legislation has been designed to ensure that
workers receive equal compensation for work of equal
value. The fact that such legislation is necessary emphasizes
the reality that barriers to fair and equitable compensation
and to career advancement do exist. These barriers may be
based on gender (commonly referred to as "The Glass
Ceiling") race, age, nationality or some other factor.

Established business organizations tend to be rigidly
structured. Acceptance of these structures and the rigidity
that accompanies them are seen as the price to be paid for
the organization's perceived stability and longevity.
Unfortunately, the structures may severely limit career
advancement and pay increases for many people. Running
a home business can represent a realistic and viable
alternative.

CASHING IN

Not too many years ago, it was often true that an employee
who worked hard would be compensated up to and beyond
retirement. Attractive as this situation may have been for
many people, it is no longer as common. Employees in all
sectors of the economy are beginning to realize that fewer
people retire from large business organizations after many

years of devoted service. As the ranks of middle management continue to be reduced, employees are reviewing their own prospects for continuous future employment.

Clearly, hearing about the dismissal of a fellow employee with more than 25 years' service forces many individuals to seriously consider their own options. As they do so, they may see their organizations in a new light. As large businesses become leaner employees may see themselves as simply a means to an end: an end that is, ultimately, bottom-line oriented.

Not surprisingly, after considering the whole picture, many of these employees may decide they neither need nor want the discomfort and uncertainty that are new features of a once enjoyable job.

For some, self-employment becomes a very realistic and viable way to replace the unease of working for a large and often impersonal organization. For many, self-employment starts with a home business.

CONTRACTING OUT

In difficult economic times, all organizations must actively seek cost-saving opportunities. Contracting out services has become a very common strategy. In essence, this involves purchasing from outside sources specific services that were formerly performed internally by employees of the organization.

Putting aside the concerns of organized labor, contracting out represents a win-win strategy for both the purchaser and the supplier of the services. The purchaser pays only for those services that are actually used.

Take, for example, the contracting out of computer programing services. Instead of paying the salary, benefits and overhead costs of maintaining full-time computer programing capability, the purchaser would pay only the cost of contracted computer programing, as these costs are incurred. Although the hourly cost may well be higher than the corresponding hourly cost if performed by employees, the total annual cost could be substantially lower. Ideally, the purchaser receives the same volume of services at a lower overall cost.

By providing services by contract, the computer programer becomes an independent contractor and may realize certain tax advantages as a result. These advantages include deducting specific expenses from business income in calculating income tax. To be deductible, the expenses must have been incurred for the purpose of generating business income.

Further, as an independent contractor, the programer could also provide services to a number of purchasers. This can, obviously, result in a significantly higher income potential than would have been possible as an employee.

As contracting out becomes more common the range of services required becomes increasingly broader. This in turn continues to increase the potential for home business.

COMPUTER TECHNOLOGY

There is no question that the current growth in home business is largely driven by advances in computer technology. Individuals who work with knowledge and with information require computers and associated telecommunications equipment, such as fax and modem machines to perform their tasks. It is this equipment, especially the computer modem, that makes it possible to communicate with others and gain access to the information highway from the home office. They need little in terms of office premises or support staff. Secretarial and other services may be purchased as needed on a fee-for-service basis.

Increasingly, people who work primarily on computers find that they usually work as well, if not better, from home than they do from organizational offices. This growth of home entrepreneurs is new and unprecedented. It is a trend that will continue to grow over the next decade.

CUTTING BACK

Just as pay equity is one of the hottest human resource issues of the decade, excess capacity must be the most widespread economic issue. There are simply too many suppliers of goods and services chasing too few clients.

The most prevalent means of dealing with this excess capacity is to cut back in every area possible. Unfortunately, cutbacks ultimately result in the termination of employees' jobs. Regardless of what the termination is called — lay off, let go, dismissal, rightsizing or early retirement — the end result is the same. Like those who chose to leave their jobs, individuals who leave involuntarily may consider self-employment in a home business as a realistic and viable option.

Once established and settled into running their own businesses, many of these people may begin to see their terminations as blessings in disguise. No longer having to follow the party line, these new entrepreneurs are free to recognize and admit the frustrations that may have formed part of the fabric of their jobs and overall work environment. Many may realize that much of their time and energy on the job was directed to following established patterns and maintaining the *status quo*. The challenge of personal growth and development, once an important driving force, had been replaced by the burden of keeping the organizational machinery moving.

In operating their own home business, many people may experience a sense of renewal. They may have a refocused sense of energy and commitment to their jobs and to their clients. Instead of seeing their terminations as crises, they may come to recognize the end of their jobs as opportunities for growth and development. For many, home businesses represent the potential for new and exciting possibilities.

2

WHAT'S RIGHT ABOUT HOME BUSINESS

There are many reasons why an individual would choose to start a home business. For the most part, these reasons are personal. They flow from the individual's lifestyle decisions and the circumstances surrounding his or her job or workplace. From a purely business perspective, there are a number of factors that make home businesses attractive operational formats.

THE EFFICIENCY EDGE

Service that is primarily delivered by a single individual is often more profitable and of higher quality if delivered from a home office. Here's why.

Today's large business organizations are products of the Industrial Revolution. Just as the economies of scale encouraged the development of larger and more automated factories, the perception that "bigger is better" encouraged the development of larger business organizations. And bigger factories and business organizations required correspondingly large volumes of capital. Many businesses came to believe that if they had enough resources — human, physical and financial — there would be virtually no limit to the volume of goods and services they could sell. That belief has been shattered.

The focus of our economy has shifted from the production of goods to the delivery of services. Today, according to the Marketing Science Institute of Cambridge, Mass., the provision of service accounts for approximately 67% of domestic Gross National Product.

Large factories and big business organizations now find themselves with extensive and expensive excess capacity. While "onward and upward" was the doctrine of the past, "downsizing" is today's credo. Survival of the organization through cost reduction often takes precedence over client service. The situation has been exacerbated by the technological revolution working in conjunction with the dawning of the information age.

Utilizing the resources of a large organization is not necessarily the only way to ensure client satisfaction. To provide exemplary service to clients, many people need only their own knowledge and access to a computer. A broad range of reasonably priced computer equipment and software is readily available. More specialized services and facilities such as telephone answering, bookkeeping and meeting rooms are available on a fee-for-service basis. In addition, a broad range of client services can be referred or sub-contracted out. Fees are based on the value of the service, not the revenue necessary to meet high overhead. Further, better quality service is often delivered because of one's freedom from such factors as organizational considerations, internal competition or conflicting career plans.

THE MANEUVERABLE EDGE

Large organizations may be likened to the luxury liner *Queen Elizabeth II*; home businesses to windsurfers. Establishing a home business requires little capital. Like the windsurfer, it requires neither a large crew nor sophisticated technology. It relies primarily on the knowledge and skills of the individual.

The simplicity of the home business makes it more maneuverable than its big business competitors. In response to changing opportunities and conditions, a home business can take prompt and decisive action. Changes in direction can usually be made without additional resources or extensive consultation. In contrast, the sheer momentum of large organizations requires a major redeployment of resources and endless consultations to effect even the smallest change. For example, it took the North American automobile industry several years to respond to their customers' demand for smaller cars.

THE INTUITIVE EDGE

The Oxford English Dictionary defines intuition as "... *the immediate apprehension . . . without the intervention of a reasoning process.*" It is the "aha" or "eureka" of a sudden insight, often experienced at the most unexpected times.

Business is rich with examples of intuition-driven success stories. Ray Kroc, well-known developer of the McDonalds Restaurant empire, is featured in one such story. In 1960 he offered to purchase the business and franchise rights from Richard and Maurice McDonald, the restaurant's original founders. The brothers quoted a price of $2.7 million and removed the original restaurant from the deal. Kroc's lawyer advised him not to pay the exorbitant price. Kroc listened to his own intuition: he called his lawyer back and said "take it." The rest, as they say, is history.

Whether it's playing a hunch or relying on good or bad feelings in making decisions, intuition is a significant and generally positive feature of our business environment.

The bad news about intuition is that it is not always a welcome feature. As discussed, today's big business organizations are legacies of the Industrial Revolution; they have developed the unshakeable belief that bigger is better. They have also been greatly influenced by the scientific method, which encourages logical, rational and provable thinking and decision making. Deviations from linear thinking are often unwelcome and unacceptable in business organizations. Although intuitive individuals may work for the biggies, they must often suppress their intuition to ensure career advancement.

Such organizations have been called "The Enemy of Intuition":

> Big organizations, and that includes governments, unions, and corporate oligopolies that submerge the individual, are clearly intuition's enemy. No boss can keep contact with everything that is going on, much less see down into the engine room of the organization where a head of anti-management steam may be building. Communication from below is expressed impersonally in numbers, plans, and analyses, and executive decisions are

based on these abstractions . . . on lower levels, intuitive ideas are automatically tuned out. Eurekas are simply not a factor, because no credence is given to anything that can't be weighed, measured, and analyzed by computer. . . [2]

The good news is that the simpler, less convoluted structure of home businesses is the ideal environment for intuition. Being able to bring to bear everything that he or she has ever seen, felt, and experienced in working with clients enables the business person to draw fully on personal intuitive forces. Intuitive ideas need not be weighed, measured or analyzed by computer; they need only to serve the client better.

THE COMPETITIVE EDGE

Home businesses are also well positioned to develop and maintain a competitive advantage over larger business operations. A more efficient and less cumbersome structure can deliver services more responsively and at lower cost than can larger businesses. The home business "windsurfer" can maneuver effectively to take advantage of new opportunities and to avoid upcoming difficulties.

The features that make home businesses so attractive in today's climate will continue to benefit some businesses in the future. Unlike the Industrial Age, in which vast amounts of capital were required to develop or acquire production tools, the Information Age will provide major opportunities for ordinary individuals with modest resources.

3

BUSINESSES THAT CAN BE OPERATED FROM THE HOME

The first home businesses, in fact the first independent businesses, were operated by skilled tradespeople and artisans. Goods of all kinds — primarily to meet personal and household needs and those of agriculture and defence — were produced from the homes of the craftspeople and sold directly to the end users. With the coming of the Industrial Revolution, enterprising individuals realized that by bringing these workers together in a common workplace, more goods could be produced at a lower per unit cost. Eventually, Henry Ford developed his assembly line and the principles of mass production became the operative business practice for most of the twentieth century.

Now, as the Industrial Age loses its momentum, we are experiencing a resurgence of interest in home businesses. Home businesses can sell products, provide services or some combination of both. The best choices require a minimum of space and equipment and focus primarily on the personal skills and ability of the business operator.

SERVICES OFFERED FROM HOME

Gathering Information

Unless the activities being observed are taking place in a controlled, in-house setting, such as market research focus groups, observation usually takes place away from a central office. Reporting the observations can be done from the observer's home office with the actual report transmitted to a central facility by telephone modem, fax machine, courier or ordinary mail.

Surveying and interviewing can be done in person or by telephone. The home office can easily serve as a base from which the surveys and interviews are planned, implemented and co-ordinated. Research findings can be analyzed in the home office with the report transmitted using almost any available technology.

Processing Information

The tasks of processing and communicating or disseminating information can all be done from a properly computerized home office. Newsletters, for example, have long been produced and distributed from home offices. The editor assembles information intended for a planned newsletter and then prepares, edits or "processes" it for ultimate inclusion. Once the newsletter has been prepared, it is distributed to readers in print or electronic form. Each aspect of disseminating information, from collection to processing to the actual dissemination itself, can be done from home.

Copying, Storing and Retrieving Information

Manual or automated record keeping, transcribing, recording and reviewing business information can easily be done from a home office. Personal computers linked in a local area network (LAN) make it possible for vast amounts of data to be easily stored and readily accessed from office or home. High rental rates for office and commercial space have led to the practice of storing closed files of hard copy material off-site in storage warehouses. If a specific file is needed, the warehouse operator is notified and one or more boxes of files is taken from the warehouse and forwarded to the office.

Whenever I have seen boxes of closed files stacked and awaiting either in-house searching or return to the warehouse, I have questioned the efficiency of the system. Surely a more efficient approach would be to dispatch a properly qualified and briefed individual to the warehouse to retrieve specific documents or information. Why couldn't qualified independent file clerks, working from home offices, retrieve and deliver individual files?

Advising or Consulting

As many practitioners are finding, these tasks are ideally suited for home businesses. Information is gathered and processed as outlined above; advice and recommendations are prepared in the home office and communicated to the client.

Training

Normally, corporate training involves an instructor conducting a specific educational program for students. The training may take place either in an in-house facility or in a rented off-site facility. Many instructors have found that they require neither in-house offices nor on-site training facilities to provide effective training. Pre-training preparation, such as designing the program, preparing the materials and teaching aids and practicing presentations may be performed in home offices. The actual training sessions may be conducted in facilities rented from private suppliers — hotels, convention centers, resorts — or from private or public educational institutions. Teaching aids such as audio-visual equipment or computers may also be rented from a broad range of suppliers. Increasingly for corporations and instructors, contracting out training services has become a common and effective approach to corporate training.

OPPORTUNITIES FOR TRADITIONAL BUSINESS OPERATIONS
Traditional business and related organizations can also reduce costs significantly by contracting services out to home-based knowledge practitioners. Again, the cost will be limited to the services purchased, since they eliminate the need for such overhead features as office space, computer equipment, secretarial and clerical services, and employee benefits. As a result, home businesses can provide cost-effective services for traditional organizations. These opportunities may be illustrated by using the following example of training services that have been contracted out to a home-based corporate trainer.

An employer has identified a specific training need: a number of new employees are below the minimal acceptable level of competence in specific software programs. To provide the required training, the employer has two basic choices.

One approach would be to provide the training in-house using existing resources: knowledgeable training personnel, and a training room properly equipped with appropriate computer equipment. This leads to questions such as: Are all these resources readily available? If so, how much will they cost? How skilled are the trainers in instructing the specific skills? How up-to-date is the computer equipment? If the resources are not readily available and the training must be scheduled for some point in the future, perhaps another option should be explored.

An alternative would be to contract the services out to a home-based trainer. The instructor, who presumably is an experienced teacher and knowledgeable about the specific software on which training is to be provided, would then proceed to book the computer-equipped training facility, prepare and conduct the training session or sessions and provide post-training support.

For the employer, there are a number of significant benefits. Instead of paying the ongoing overhead and development costs of trainers qualified and equipped to teach state-of-the-art skills, training costs are limited to the services purchased when and as needed. Personnel training in all areas has become so important and costly that it is no longer reasonable to expect that in-house training resources can remain current, and by extension effective. It is usually preferable to hire experienced outside instructors who are knowledgeable about current skills than to entrust training to less experienced and less up-to-date in-house trainers.

The same principles apply beyond the training room. Whether computer programming or writing newsletters, there is now a broad range of functions that may be delivered effectively and efficiently by home businesses.

The downsizing of big business, government and not-for-profit organizations has been matched in part by an amazing growth in numbers and diversity of home business operations. Many of these former employees now operate their own businesses at home providing the same service that they formerly provided exclusively to their employers. This provides traditional business and non-business operations with new opportunities to obtain services more quickly and less expensively.

OPPORTUNITIES FOR ARTISTS AND CRAFTSPEOPLE

These creative people compromise a very unique group of information and knowledge practitioners. Information about various art forms such as acting, ceramics, dressmaking, painting or writing is widely available.

What separates the true artist from the "wannabe" artist is a thorough understanding of how specific information is applied in practice. This knowledge of body movements and voice projection, or of combining colors or words, comes from extensive training and practice. The skill — or knowledge — of the artist lies in applying specific information to create a unique and beautiful work. As vital as information about specific art forms is, it is only when this information is applied that a work of art is created.

GOODS MANUFACTURED AT HOME

Most manufacturing operations require too much capital or are too labor intensive to be viable home business operations. Economic considerations apart, few of us would voluntarily turn our homes into factories. Production operations involving any or all of high-volume, sophisticated production operations and a large work force are best left to large industrial organizations.

On the other hand, the production of unique high-quality arts and crafts is ideally suited to a home business operation. Examples would include such traditional crafts as dressmaking, jewelry making, pottery and woodworking. With products such as these, the emphasis should be on the uniqueness and the quality of the work produced. With effective marketing strategies, producers of unique, high-quality goods will continue to be successful.

GOODS MANUFACTURED BY OTHERS

Many successful home businesses involve the distribution of products manufactured by others. Typical businesses fit into the distribution chain anywhere from purchasing directly from the manufacturer to purchasing from sub-distributors and selling to the end user. Examples of these businesses include distributing cosmetics, jewelry, cleaning supplies and various other products manufactured elsewhere.

Distributing the products of others can be done in a variety of ways; all involve **wholesalers, distributors** and **retailers** who purchase goods for resale. Their income is generated by selling the goods at a higher price than they paid for them. These people must pay for the goods they purchase for resale, regardless of whether they succeed in selling them.

Franchises have been described as the most successful marketing concept ever created.

> Franchising is a system that businesses choose to expand their operations . . . rather than draw on their own capital to finance the expansion, franchisors rely on franchisees who invest their own money to open and operate the business . . . Three elements define a franchise company: (1) use of a trade name or trade

mark; (2) payment of fees and royalties; and (3) significant control or assistance provided by the franchisor.[3]

The assistance provided by the franchisor makes a franchise an attractive business format for the novice home business operator. Suitable areas include beauty and health products, business, computer, education, maintenance, photography and publicity. Franchise fees can range from several hundred dollars to hundreds of thousands of dollars to acquire franchise rights. These rights include the right to use a trade name or trademark, an exclusive territory, training in the management and operations of the franchised business, marketing support and the right to distribute the franchisor's products. Often the franchisees pay a percentage of their sales revenues, in the form of royalties to the franchisor.

Dozens of directories and handbooks are available in public libraries and book stores that detail various franchise opportunities. These resources also outline what to look for and what to avoid in purchasing a franchise. *The Best Home-Based Franchises* by Gregory Matusky and the Philip Lief Group is one of the more helpful resources for would-be franchisees. The book is listed in Chapter 18.

Another growing trend is the use of **multi-level marketing**. As the name suggests, this involves a number of different levels of distributors. The manufacturer sells products to a high-level distributor, who in turn resells the products to the next lower level of distributor, and so on, until ultimately the products are sold to the end user. Such companies as Amway, Mary Kaye Cosmetics and Tupperware are typical multi-level marketing arrangements.

Like multi-level marketing, **network marketing** is

based on the premise that satisfied users of specialty products will want to sell the products to their relatives and acquaintances. Essentially, network marketers act as resellers of the products that they claim to enjoy using. Our current interest in health and fitness has helped launch networks marketing a broad range of health and beauty products such as those supplied by Herb-a-Life and Body-Wise.

Contemporary advances in communications technology and courier services have increased the attractiveness and profitability of businesses based on multi-level and network marketing. Among the most attractive features of these business formats is the broad range of operating and marketing support provided by the manufacturers or suppliers of the products.

Another approach to distribution of goods is to act as a **manufacturer's representative or agent**. In this case, the representative never actually owns the products; he or she take orders for the manufacturer or supplier and is paid by commission. Unless otherwise agreed, commissions are payable when the supplier receives payment for the goods sold.

Trading in collectibles and memorabilia is ideally suited for home businesses. Growing nostalgia has given new life to the expression that "everything old is new again." Collecting and reselling almost anything that is old — furniture, jewelry, books, newspapers, trading cards, clothes and so on — has become a major source of revenue for a large number of individuals.

A fixed place of business is not only unnecessary, but is often restrictive. Shows, fairs, exhibitions and sales can be found at the nearest shopping center, at downtown and suburban hotels and at flea markets everywhere. The stock-in-trade is hauled from home (or storage) to the show, set up and offered for sale. Unsold items return to home base to await the next sale. The management and administrative work is usually completed at home offices.

The fact that we live in a global village now means that regardless of where products are manufactured — locally, nationally, or internationally — they can usually be easily obtained for distribution from a home business. Opportunities to import or distribute products manufactured by others can be found in virtually any classified advertising section of any newspaper. Business opportunities can also be identified through leisure travel. Ideas and concepts that appear to be working effectively in distant locations can often be implemented at home.

SUPPLYING SERVICES

If service is defined as "any act or labor that one person does for another that does not result in the ownership of anything tangible," it is clear that service is a component of all but the most basic of goods. However, it is useful to think of services as distinct from goods or products.

The "service sector" has experienced an extraordinary rate of growth over the past decade. In the past ten years, 94% of all new jobs in the U.S.A. and Canada were created by the service industries — retailing, business and financial services, engineering and design, consulting, commercial education and training, communication, travel and transportation.

Services may be classified by identifying the end user who can be an individual, a group, an organization or another business.

Personal Services Provided To Individuals

These services are defined by the personal needs, wants and expectations of the person to whom the service is being provided. Generally speaking, the services are tasks that could be undertaken and completed by the recipient of the services if he or she had the time, talent and inclination.

Traditionally, personal services have included beauty and fashion-related services such as hairstyling and make-up. With the growth of two-income families, who often trade off more money with less time, tasks usually performed by individuals for themselves have been "contracted out" to others. As a result, new service opportunities proliferate at a staggering rate. Many successful businesses now profitably provide services such as housekeeping, care-giving, home maintenance and gardening. If you are too busy to shop, you can hire a shopping service to do it for you. If you have no time to plan a party or family event, a number of professional party planners would be more than pleased to assist. Yellow Page directories list hundreds of personal services ranging from Acupuncuturists through Makeup Artists to Yoga Instruction.

New business opportunities continue to arise in response to society's changing needs. One extreme example is the service provided by a Japanese company with the intriguing name of Japan Efficiency Headquarters. This company has developed a unique concept of providing personal services. It rents professional actors to visit elderly parents in the place of their busy adult offspring. The actors serve as stand-ins for family visits, allowing the older family members to maintain some form of contact with their younger "family."

Because of its "portability" a home business is ideal for providing personal services. Having acquired the requisite skills and tools of the trade, the business operator can adopt the hired gunslinger's motto: "Have Tools, Will Travel." Services are delivered where the client needs and wants them. Management and routine administrative tasks are completed at the home office.

Services Provided to Business and Other Organizations
Businesses and non-profit associations purchase services for one of two reasons. The first is the simplest and most basic: to meet their own organizational needs and to operate and maintain the business. The second is to acquire new information and/or knowledge.

Services of the first type would include obtaining and delivering inventory and supplies, running errands, taking messages, maintaining books and records and cleaning business premises. All business operations require these services to some extent; few require them on a full-time basis. Since they require minimal equipment and space, such services can readily be provided by a home business.

In many cases, the home business operator hires other people to do the actual work involved in providing the service. For example, other people obtain and deliver inventory and supplies, perform the bookkeeping tasks, etc. These people are paid less to perform the work than the client is charged for the service. Profit comes from the difference between the actual cost of providing the service and the fees charged to the client.

In hiring other people to provide services, the role of the home business operator shifts. Instead of actually providing the services, he or she co-ordinates and supervises the delivery of services. Again, although the actual services may be provided at the clients' place of business, the management and administration necessary to provide the services can be performed in a home office.

4

WHY HOME BUSINESS WILL THRIVE

We are living in a very challenging age. It seems as though our entire world is changing at an unprecedented rate. It is nearly impossible to keep up with the latest trends. How can anyone understand the present, let alone forecast the future?

Fortunately, assistance is available from many sources. Among them is Faith Popcorn, who, in her best-selling book *The Popcorn Report*,[4] predicts what we will buy, where we will work and what we will think in the 1990s and beyond. Her own business was started from and operates on what she learned from her family's small business. Her company's client list includes many of the world's leading business organizations.

In his best selling work *The Knowledge Value Revolution*,[5] Taichi Sakaiya prophesies a new economic and social order. Sakaiya, born in Tokyo, was a civil servant before becoming a writer and commentator of great influence in Japan and, increasingly, around the world.

What do these writers have to say about the present and the future that has significance for home businesses? *The*

Popcorn Report[6] outlines ten trends, four of which have direct relevance here.

Cocooning

The term was initially coined to mean ". . . the impulse to go inside when it just gets too tough and scary outside. To pull a shell of safety around yourself so that you're not at the mercy of a mean unpredictable world . . ."[6] The increasing number of home businesses is evidence of this trend. And as these businesses grow in number and scope, so will their credibility in the eyes of current and potential clients.

Egonomics

Using the word "ego" — the individual — as its base, this trend indicates that ". . . everybody wants a little more attention, a little recognition of the 'no one is quite like me' self . . ."[7]

No longer satisfied with driving the same model black car, customers demand a wide range of models in a wide range of colors. Ironically, providing such choices eliminates the benefits to be gained from standardized mass production. Is it merely a coincidence that automobile manufacturers were losing vast amounts of money while at the same time increasing the range of models available? The maneuverability of home businesses enables them to respond more effectively and efficiently to clients' demand for individual recognition.

Cashing In

This is the trend to ". . . slow down your racing heartbeat and revive your weary soul . . . It's cashing in the career chips you've been stacking up these years and going somewhere else to work at something you want to do, the way you want to do it."[8] The Industrial Age drew workers from their homes to factories and offices. The end of the Industrial Age may mean that more individuals will work from their homes. This will increase the number and diversity of home businesses. Through selective networking and referrals, home businesses can provide a broad range of services to clients.

Vigilante Consumer

This trend is best described in Faith Popcorn's own words:

> It's an action adventure story that strikes terror in the hearts of corporations everywhere (or should). Our heroine, one timid and trusting Tillie Consumer, changes her name to Attila and strikes out at evil in supermarkets and the marketing world everywhere: attacking trickery, hype, and sham with all the weapons she has at hand: her telephone, her typewriter, her increasingly powerful pocketbook . . . The consumer is fighting back . . .[9]

Being closer to their clients, home businesses are less likely to alienate Attila and find themselves subject to her wrath. Indeed, they may be the beneficiaries of this wrath. If big organizations are seen to be bad, smaller opportunities might be seen as preferable alternatives.

From a different and broader perspective, Taichi Sakaiya observes and records many trends. Most are global with little direct application to home business operations. Two trends are, however, significant and worthy of note.

Light/Thin/Short/Small

"The prevailing outlook changed as the 1980s began.

'Light/Thin/Short/Small' was the slogan that defined a new aesthetic that made light, compact products all the rage. Suddenly the era when 'big' and 'beautiful' were practically synonyms was at an end."[10] As a result of reduced demand, excess capacity, increased competition and decreased profits, we have seen large organizations in every economic sector undertake massive downsizing. Home businesses are the ultimate downsized business operation. They are very much a part of this trend; they will continue to thrive as the trend continues.

Research Trends

"Current research and development . . . tends to revolve around finding new ways to save energy, to create more adaptable and multifunctional products and to disseminate information."[11]

Home businesses are consistent with each of these research objectives. Working at home instead of traveling to traditional office premises requires less energy. Home offices represent very adaptable and multifunctional uses of resources, resources integrally involved in the dissemination of information.

Global Restructuring

Many observers have commented that we are not recovering from a worldwide recession; we are in fact experiencing a major restructuring. The surprising collapse of the Berlin Wall followed by the equally surprising collapse of the Soviet Union and the changes in South Africa attest to this "new world order."

No country or business operation is exempt from this widespread desire for change. Large organizations, such as General Motors, formerly thought to be secure forever, have scrambled to find workable survival strategies. Despite continuing high profit levels, banks and financial institutions struggle to deal with increasing numbers of problem loans to former blue chip clients.

Taken collectively, these trends do not auger well for the traditional ways of doing things. As stated, there is ample evidence to suggest that the approaches that have worked so well in the past are not working as well now and may not work at all in the future.

New ways of doing things must be found. One of the most exciting and viable new approaches to profitable business operation is the home business. Enjoying an annual growth rate of 12%, as reported by *Entrepreneur* magazine, home businesses will surely be a major force in the future.

5

QUALITY SERVICE: A CRITICAL BUSINESS STRATEGY

At Ford, Quality Is Job 1 and It's Working.

At Zenith, The Quality Goes In Before The Name Goes On.

At McDonalds, Quality is Guaranteed.

Quality is the most important strategic issue facing top management in the 1990s. What we mean by quality is more than the traditional notion of quality in products and services . . . It is a bottom line issue that addresses the very roots of a business, and it requires a change in thinking from the top of an organization to the bottom. To put it succinctly, there is a strong correlation between quality and profitability.[12]

Modern principles of quality management were first introduced in Japan following World War II. As a result, the Japanese economy has grown from post-war devastation to global pre-eminence. Many North American companies have followed the Japanese lead in trying to manage quality. Some organizations have found it to be a very effective operating philosophy.

For most large organizations, all this talk about quality remains just that: talk. Despite the boldest intentions, and the expenditure of millions of dollars, the general culture and individual environments of large organizations seem anti-quality. The management structure of many business organizations is such that their employees couldn't deliver quality client service — even if they wanted to. In trying to provide quality service to clients, employees are often caught between supervisors whose personal agendas focus on self-preservation, and inadequately trained support staff who may not know the meaning of quality.

For the home business, the significant element of the above quotation is the sentence "... *To put it succinctly, there is a strong correlation between quality and profitability.*" Free from non-supportive supervisors and support staff, home businesses strive to ensure quality client service to all clients, all of the time. In fact, the quality of client service can actually be better than that of larger competitors.

The "flavor-of-the-month" world of current business theory has spawned innumerable experts on the subject of quality. Since 1990, more than 300 books have been written on the subject — in North America alone! Every major business and trade publication has devoted considerable space to the importance of and role of quality. A whole new jargon has developed; phrases like Acceptable Quality Level (AQL), Continuous-Improvement Process (CIP), and Quality Function Deployment (QFD) abound.

In short, quality has become the "snake oil" of the decade, the cure-all for all manner of management problems — low revenues, high costs, fierce competition, low staff morale. The rationale behind this approach seems to be that if quality management worked so well in post-war

Japan, despite that country's overwhelming problems and lack of resources, it should work even better for us with fewer (or at least different) problems and more resources.

Today, all business organizations profess a commitment to quality. Many have implemented some kind of formal program of quality management. Many of these organizations have succeeded in their endeavors. Those that have tend to be smaller and flatter in organizational structure with an overall operating philosophy that encourages employee participation and team work.

Not surprisingly, today's widespread interest in quality yields significant benefits to smaller businesses in general and home businesses in particular. This focus can, in fact, give a substantial competitive advantage to home businesses.

As we shift from the product-oriented marketplace of the Industrial Age to the service-oriented market of the Information Age, the importance of the service component attached to products becomes increasingly important. Products are sold on the basis of services promised and delivered. The duration of the power train warranty on a new automobile is almost as important a selling point as the performance of the power train itself.

The service component of products sold by home businesses is equally important. Indeed, it is the service component that often distinguishes products provided by home businesses from those provided by larger businesses. Personal service at home from a knowledgeable Avon, Fuller Brush or Tupperware representative may prove superior to the uninformed indifference often displayed by clerks in larger shopping centers and department stores.

Regardless of the product provided by the home business, the quality of the service accompanying the product is vitally important. For the most part, the home business environment is free of the factors that make quality service so difficult for large organizations. I became acutely aware of this after I left the major professional services firm for which I had been working. While with the firm, the decision whether I should accept specific consulting assignments was guided by considerations such as: "How important is this client to the firm (or more likely my supervisor and his personal career plan)?;" "How much revenue is this client likely to contribute this month? this year?;" and "What other business could this client refer to our firm?" Operating my business from my home office, the consider-ations became: "What does this client need, want and expect from me?;" "Do I have the resources to profitably meet these needs and wants?;" and "What is the client will-ing to pay for this service?" Because corporate agendas and supervisors' career plans no longer exist for home business owners, they cease to be obstacles to quality client services. The common sense principles of quality client service are free to operate.

The following three chapters address these principles. The basic concepts are as simple and inexpensive to imple-ment in home businesses as they are complex and costly to realize in large organizations.

6

TEN BASIC TRUTHS ABOUT CLIENT SERVICE

Although there may be some similarities, providing clients with service is dramatically different from providing them with goods. The following truths outline the main differences.

1. Clients don't want the service itself; they want the benefits of the service.
This is particularly true of most professional services. Except for the occasional person who thrives on the attention that comes from medical treatment or court actions, most clients aren't thrilled with spending time, energy and money visiting their dentist or auto body shop.

What clients really want are the *benefits* that come from the service. These benefits may include help in resolving a problem or assistance in acquiring information, or even purchasing knowledge or skills that they lack. For example, the benefits of dental services would be healthier, more attractive teeth. Similarly, the benefits of time-consuming auto body shop services might include the repair and use of a damaged motor vehicle.

2. Clients need your service.

Customers usually consider their internal resources before looking elsewhere to purchase services. This means that you are not your clients' first choice. They need you to perform some task that they are unwilling or unable to perform for themselves.

Thus, the services that you ultimately deliver to your clients are defined by their own needs. Services could be the performance of specific tasks such as writing an operations manual or preparing advertising copy. Alternatively, the services could involve providing specialized information and knowledge such as a summary of attractive investments. In many cases, the services involve both providing information and performing specific tasks, such as summarizing potential investments and then purchasing investments on the client's behalf.

3. Clients demand quality service.

As noted in the previous chapter, the demand for quality service is widespread in contemporary society. This demand is just as commonplace with business people as it is with consumers, and results from two forces working simultaneously.

Business people are also consumers. Like everyone else, they are bombarded with advertising that emphasizes quality as a vital component of fast food, cars, home appliances, housing, travel accommodations and so forth. The message is bound to spill over into their work. If quality is an important component of their personal lives, then shouldn't it also be a component of their work lives? If the products they purchase as consumers are "quality checked," why should they settle for anything less at work?

The second force is the increasing number of business organizations currently adopting formal quality programs. Total Quality Management, or TQM, is becoming one of the most popular buzz-words of the 90s. A key TQM principle requires suppliers, e.g., you and your competitors, to provide evidence of your ability to deliver quality goods and services to your clients. Failure to provide this evidence will put you at a serious disadvantage when competing with those who can.

4. Quality service is what your clients say it is.

Many retail businesses have posted signs with the following rules of customer service:

> **Rule #1:** The client is always right.
> **Rule #2:** If you think the client is wrong, read Rule #1.

This is one way of defining quality service. If your standards of quality coincide with or exceed your clients' standards, you will be successful. If your standards fail to meet those of your clients, you risk losing their business.

A cautionary note: Clients' standards for one reason or another may be unrealistic. They may not fully understand what they require from you. They may also not fully understand what you can and cannot do for them. It is your responsibility to ensure that the client understands your services and the standards of quality that may be reasonably expected.

5. Providing technical information is not quality service.

Generally speaking, most clients are looking for more than technical information.

For example, when I consider purchasing new software for my computer system, I want to know whether the software will perform specific functions. I am not looking for a lecture on the technical specifications of the latest version of the piece of software. Quality service in this situation consists of listening to what I am asking, and applying whatever technical information may be relevant to answering my questions in terms that I can understand. Like most consumers, I am usually ready to purchase when I understand what I am buying and what benefits I will receive.

The same principles apply regardless of the field. Do not simply recite technical information to clients: draw on your knowledge to help them understand how the technical information can be applied in their unique situations. Ensure that your clients fully understand the benefits that can reasonably be expected as a result of your service.

6.   Clients do not always understand your technical jargon. As we become more familiar with technical information we learn to communicate with our colleagues and peers in a form of oral shorthand or jargon. Consultants perform "SWOT analyses," financial analysts "crunch some numbers," "psychologists administer a "WISC-III," and so on. To those in the know, the meaning of these terms is perfectly clear. To the uninitiated, they are gobbledygook. Communicating with clients involves treading a fine line between using terminology that is too technical, and talking down to the client by using language that is too simple. It is vitally important to listen carefully to each client — as an individual.

Knowing your client will enable you to assess what he or she knows now and what he or she needs to learn in order to make a decision. This will also enable you to frame your questions and comments in terms that your client will understand fully.

7. Standardized technical services will produce comparable results, regardless of the provider of the service.

This is true of every standardized service area. Various insurance brokers will provide policies with analogous features. Although independent, they act as sales agents for the same insurance companies. Similarly, assuming they follow the same procedures for the same purposes, independent researchers will produce similar results. They are after all, considering the same information base.

The farther one moves away from standardized services, the easier it becomes to distinguish services amongst competing businesses. Those services of individual consultants are often defined by their unique skills, knowledge and experience. Thus, two individual consultants may offer quite different but equally workable solutions for the same problem. The best solution is clearly the one that works best for the client.

8. Client service is intangible.

As noted, services are intangible: they cannot be seen, tasted, felt, heard or smelled before they are purchased. This means that clients who are considering the purchase of services must draw inferences of quality indirectly.

In the case of large organizations, this means looking at physical premises, personnel, equipment, communications material, symbols and logos and the price of the service. In home businesses, the range is limited to you, your communications material, your symbols and logos and your pricing. Obviously, with fewer criteria on which you're being evaluated, you must strive to exceed client expectations.

9. Customer service is variable.

Because service cannot be mass produced on an assembly

line, the same service can vary from one provider to another. Although it is true that all hair stylists receive the same basic training, it is unlikely each one would create the identical hair style for a specific client.

In less standard service areas such as consulting, there is considerable variance from practitioner to practitioner. With no uniform training and continuing education standards, consultants are free to provide whatever services they believe will sell. In situations like this, any standardization or consistency of service standards occurs more by coincidence than design.

10. Client service is perishable.
Services cannot be produced and stored in inventory until they are needed. They are produced and used virtually simultaneously. This often results in service providers experiencing significant peaks and valleys in workload — and revenue — during the year. For example, businesses that prepare tax returns face high demand for their services between February and April and low demand between July and September.

7

WHAT ARE CLIENTS REALLY LOOKING FOR?

Simple answers to complex questions are sometimes found in the most unexpected places at the most unexpected times. As I considered the question, I felt intimidated by the mountains of market research that have accumulated on the topic. As the task of analyzing and digesting this mass of material grew more onerous, I did what most reasonable people would do: I abandoned the chore and went on to do something else. It was while I was doing other things that I had a flash of insight from a seemingly unrelated source.

I recalled a situation in which I was working with a client who was struggling to keep his small bakery operating. As my client outlined his complex predicament, I became overwhelmed by the task of finding solutions to his problems. There was hardly an area in which he wasn't facing serious problems: his bank and suppliers were pushing him for money; his clients were demanding more varied and better quality products; he thought that one of his employees was stealing from him; and as if to confuse the situation even further, his wife was threatening to leave him if things didn't improve. Although he came to me for advice, I didn't know which of the problems had the highest priority, let alone what advice to give.

In desperation, I took a step that seemed most unusual for professionals in general, and for advisors in particular. I simply asked him what he wanted. After recovering from the shock, he was able to articulate an answer: he wanted to bake bread.

In hindsight, I realized that my part in the discussion was to help my client identify what he was looking for and to help him understand what I could and could not do for him. As a result, we developed the ideal service situation: I knew what he wanted and he knew what I could do. From that point, I was able to help him arrange his priorities.

To do so, I directed my client's thinking through properly formulated and focused questions. Open-ended questions, not answerable with a simple 'yes', or 'no', allowed my client to discuss his situation with few constraints. Closed questions, requiring a simple 'yes' or, 'no', answer, allowed me to focus on specific issues. As a result, I was able to gather all the information about the client and his situation that was necessary to develop and implement a proper course of action. (When I last spoke with him, he was happily working as a baker in a small resort hotel owned and operated by friends of his new spouse.)

Knowledge

Your clients will come to you because they have a problem or issue with which they need help. They are looking for two types of knowledge. First, they need to know what you can and cannot do to help them. Be honest with yourself and your client. If you can help, tell them what you can do. Conversely, if you cannot help them, offer to assist them in finding someone who can.

Secondly, they need your knowledge, or ability to create new knowledge, about their unique situation. This is what you will ultimately be selling to them. If the client had the knowledge or ability, it is unlikely that he or she would be coming to you in the first place.

Reliability

This is the ability to provide what you promised to your client dependably and accurately. This could be as simple as calling the client at an arranged hour on a specific day or as complex as providing a detailed review before a strict deadline. Clients rarely expect the moon — they are not stupid; they know what you can and cannot deliver. They do, however, expect you to deliver, dependably and accurately, what you have promised.

Responsiveness

Clients expect you to be willing to help them and to provide timely service. If your service is not prompt, you will not remain in business for long.

Assurance

Assurance is the result of your knowledge and courtesy combined with your ability to convey trustworthiness and confidence. When first meeting with my clients, I have learned to allow them to have their say. As well as appearing knowledgeable and interested, you can gain valuable insights from listening to clients convey their problems in a seemingly undirected manner. Very often, remaining objective enables you to develop a solution to the problem as you listen.

When asking questions, use words and terms that you know your clients will understand. Your approach should be conversational rather than adversarial. The purpose of the questions is to obtain information from your client, not to prove that you are right and he or she is wrong. There is little to be gained by winning the argument but losing the client.

Empathy

Empathy is reflected in the degree of caring and individual attention you provide to a client. Although perhaps the most important expectation to meet, this is often the most neglected.

The simplest method of demonstrating that you care about your clients is to really listen to them. Don't just try to impress clients with jargon and self-serving monologues. Ask questions to help your clients better understand what they may need from you.

Operating your business from home can give you a significant advantage in providing individual attention to clients. Because you will usually meet your clients away from your own place of business, you will be free of distracting telephone calls and other interruptions that are common in traditional business settings. Thus you should be able to devote all of your attention to the client.

Tangibles

This refers to your appearance and that of everything that you use and produce in dealing with clients. Once again, you may have a distinct advantage over larger businesses. You determine how you should dress to meet with clients. You also have total control over the appearance of your tools and your work. You are able to prepare and present all written material the way you think looks best. You have full responsibility for presenting yourself and your work as competent, professional and sensitive to client needs.

WHAT CLIENTS ARE NOT LOOKING FOR

- Lectures on how their problems could have been prevented. 20/20 hindsight is of little use to anyone.
- Monologues and anecdotes that serve only to feed your ego and demonstrate how smart you think you are.
- Unrealistic promises that cannot possibly be kept.
- Excuses for promises that were not kept.
- Indifferent and/or slow responses to requests.
- Your concerns about your lack of knowledge.
- Interrogation and arguments.

8

WHAT YOU CAN DO FOR YOUR CLIENT

The previous three chapters addressed quality in general and how it relates to clients and their expectations. This chapter outlines how you can meet these expectations.

DELIVER QUALITY SERVICE

Here are five steps that will help you ensure you consistently deliver quality service to your clients.

1. Listen to your clients.

Your clients know their respective businesses better than you do. They also know their problems better than you do. What they may not know is how to describe their problems to you. And they probably don't know what you can do to help them.

As mentioned, you can learn a great deal by listening carefully to your clients. Through careful questioning you can help them isolate their problems so that you can help develop a solution. You can also learn what your clients need to know about you.

2. Identify and meet your clients' needs.

Remember that your clients come to you because they require your assistance in meeting a specific need. Don't assume that just because you have identified a need, it is the one with which the client seeks assistance. The needs that you have identified and perceive as being important may not be the same needs your client considers crucial.

Once you have agreed on your clients' needs, it is time to discuss a plan of action. This should include what you will and will not do, what the client will do, how long you expect the process to take, and how much you expect it will cost. It is prudent to over-estimate time and expense; this allows for flexibility in case of unexpected complications and lessens the likelihood of unpleasant or embarrassing surprises.

3. Exceed clients' expectations.

Your client will now have a set of expectations regarding the delivery of your service. Just as you commit yourself to meeting your client's needs, you should make a commitment to yourself to exceed these expectations. This means providing the service better, faster or less expensively than the client expected.

4. Eliminate variables.

This step presents a significant challenge. On the one hand, the client expects and deserves unique non-standard service.

On the other hand, standardizing non-client service factors makes for greater efficiency and profitability. These factors include formats for reports and correspondence, procedures for gathering and analyzing information and practices involving billing and collecting accounts. It is not necessary, nor is it profitable, to continuously re-invent the wheel.

5. Continuously improve your service.

As a service provider, you are only as good as the last service you provided. Regardless of how well things went, undoubtedly there were areas for improvement. Using the material in Chapter 14, ask for your clients' opinions as to how your service can be improved. Other businesses, from automobile manufacturers to restaurant operators use client input to help improve service. You should follow their lead.

PROVIDE APPROPRIATE KNOWLEDGE AND SKILLS

The technological revolution and information explosion which have combined to open the door to home offices have also given rise to "instant experts." With access to an astounding volume of information, these individuals profess expertise in a broad range of areas. They often fail to realize that clients have access to the same information. What your clients really need is the knowledge or skills that renders specific information applicable to their unique situations.

Your client doesn't need you repeating information to her; she needs, for example, your knowledge of how current legislation or government regulations directly apply to her. She already knows about the importance of client satisfaction; she needs your skills to help train her employees in new approaches to customer service.

DELIVER WHAT YOU PROMISE; DON'T PROMISE WHAT YOU CAN'T DELIVER

As consumers, we are exposed to more than 3,000 commercial messages daily. Most promise worthwhile benefits if we purchase a particular product or service. Unfortunately, many of these promises seem undeliverable.

Regardless of its ultimate brightness and whiteness, a clean laundry is unlikely to result in a happier family. Drinking the right beer is not likely to dramatically improve one's social life or overall enjoyment of life. And so it goes: buy this product and your life will be measurably better. Consumers have become wary of all this hype.

Clients, consumers themselves, are often cynical when it comes to promises. They may not believe you when you promise anything. Promise whatever you choose — the proof is in the delivery. The same strategy that applies to client expectations (ensure they are reasonable and then exceed them) applies to promises. Ensure that your promises are realistic and then deliver more (better or faster). After you have developed a good track record, you will have won your client's trust — and future business.

Of course, the corollary to this rule is not to promise what you can't delivery. Ensure that your promises match your abilities and resources.

ENSURE TIMELINESS OF SERVICE

Our modern conveniences have moved from the labor-saving stage to the instant age. Instant-on television sets eliminate the few seconds of warm-up time required by conventional sets. Thanks to microwave ovens, we can enjoy gourmet macaroni and cheese in 4 minutes rather than the more usual 7 minutes. Facsimile machines enable us to communicate written information instantly. We have come to expect instant gratification of our wants and needs.

These same expectations spill over into the area of service delivery. Thanks to advanced computer technology in the business world, clients can have instant access to a staggering array of information and services. This creates intense pressure on those who provide client services. Clients have low tolerance for slow responses. Telephones must be answered promptly; telephone calls must be returned as soon as possible. Appointments must be scheduled and kept promptly.

Exacerbating the pressure, telecommunication technology has given us the tools to keep in touch wherever we travel. Clearly, it is more important than ever to ensure your clients receive timely service. This includes each client contact from telephone calls to written correspondence and reports. Time frames should be established for those services that cannot be provided immediately. Once deadlines have been set, you should make every effort to ensure they are kept.

In setting priorities and establishing deadlines you should practice the principles of effective time management. Matters that are both important and urgent always receive top priority. Although filing income tax returns is always important, in April the task becomes urgent as well.

Next in priority come matters that must be dealt with urgently. These generally require some form of crisis management as a preliminary step to final resolution. In April a sense of urgency accompanies the task of filing the tax return prepared in January that remains unfiled.

Last in priority are those matters that are important but not yet urgent. Left unattended, these matters have the tendency to become important *and* urgent. The important task of gathering information necessary to prepare your income tax returns can be done on an ongoing basis thus avoiding the sense of urgency that would otherwise develop if left until the filing deadline.

Remember that timeliness does not always mean

instant service. In every case, you and your client should come to a common understanding of what timeliness means.

ADD VALUE TO STANDARD SERVICES

The best method of distinguishing your standardized services for those of your competitors is to add something of value. Added value could take the form of additional service or information. For example, automobile manufacturers add value to the purchase of a new car by providing roadside assistance plans. Similarly, drug stores record the history of their clients' prescriptions and use this record to provide health advice and safeguards. The nature of the value that you add to your service depends upon your own resources and creativity.

The table opposite is intended as a starting point in identifying opportunities to add value to your own services.

For maximum effectiveness, these value-added services should meet the following three criteria:

Brief:	They should be concise, supplemental services to your clients. They should not overshadow your standard services.
Accurate:	Providing wrong or misleading advice or recommendations not only negates the value-added service but reduces the credibility of your standard services.
Relevant:	Your value-added services must be relevant to your client and his/her situation; again, an awareness of client needs is essential.

Typical Service	Standard Service	Suggested Value-Added Service
Accounting/ Bookkeeping	Preparing financial records and statements	Advising on increasing revenue, decreasing costs
Analyzing Investments	Identifying strengths and weaknesses of investments	Clarifying personal financial goals
Computer Programming	Preparing unique computer programs	Advising on related packaged software
Desktop Publishing	Preparing camera-ready material for printing	Recommending reliable artist for custom artwork
Editing	Correcting/improving written copy	Suggesting suitable layout and design
Management Consulting	Assisting to improve management effectiveness	Suggesting suitable marketing opportunities
Newsletter Publishing	Publishing and distributing newsletters	Recommending additional sources of information
Selling products	Distributing products	Ensuring customer knows benefits of the product
Training	Training others in personal or business skills	Recommending sources of advanced training
Typing	Preparing reports and documents	Editing and correcting spelling and grammar

PART II

DOWN TO BASICS

9

WHAT YOU NEED TO START YOUR HOME BUSINESS

Successful businesses are client-driven. This means your business must be based on using your skills and resources to satisfy other people's needs. Before starting to plan your business, you must be certain that there are specific needs in the marketplace that you can meet. Once you have done this, identify resources that you have or can acquire that will help you meet these needs. Step One in the preparation of your marketing plan in Chapter 12 will help with this process.

Awareness of Your Own Needs
Once you have identified what your clients need from you, and are satisfied that you can meet these needs, you must determine what you will require to operate your business. The following checklist outlines some standard requirements.

START-UP CHECKLIST
In the first column indicate whether you need the item. In the second column, estimate the initial or one-time start-up cost of that item. In the third column, estimate ongoing monthly expenses.

Item	Required	Start-Up Cost	Monthly Cost
Business Plan			
Business Name			
Office Area			
Office Furniture			
Things You Will Need: telephone			
answering machine			
answering service			
computer			
printer			
fax machine			
copier			
cellular telephone			
pager			
line manager			
modem			
Specialized Equipment			
Office Supplies			
Software: wordprocessing			
spreadsheet			
accounting			
contact/customer data base			
project management			
desktop publishing			

Stationery:	business cards			
	letterhead			
	envelopes			
	other			
Automobile				
Licenses, permits, etc.				
Tax registrations:	Sales Tax			
	Income Tax			
	other			
Membership Fees				
Insurance:	Property			
	Liability			
	Life			
	Disability			
Banking Services:	Chequing account			
	Line of credit			
	Credit card			
	Other			
Accountant				
Lawyer				
Other				
Total Start-Up Costs Monthly Expenses				

By adding the second and third columns, you can estimate your initial or start-up costs and your monthly operating expenses. These figures will be used in preparing your business plan.

Business Plan

Although many businesses try to operate without a plan, few succeed in the long run. Your plan will determine your goals and identify the strategies to follow in achieving them. The development of a business plan is set out in Chapter 11.

Business Name

As a rule, if you conduct business in a name other than your own, you must register that name with the appropriate government department. Registration is usually a very simple process. You can and should do it yourself. Obviously, the name of your business should accurately reflect your services.

It may be advantageous for you to incorporate your business. In addition to limiting your personal liability, incorporation offers a number of tax advantages. These include reduced income tax on the corporation and a greater potential for income splitting between you and your spouse. You should discuss these possible advantages with your accountant. If you do incorporate, you can do this work yourself. There are many helpful books and publications available through government sources, book stores and libraries that will help you.

Office Area

The best home office space is the one that works best for you and your family. It's your choice — select the office space that you think will be comfortable for you and acceptable to other members of the household.

If used primarily for business purposes, your home office space becomes a tax-deductible expense. Simply calculate the percentage of the total floor space of your home occupied by your office. This percentage of house occupancy costs — taxes, utilities, maintenance — becomes a tax deductible expense. Check with your accountant or tax advisor for further clarification.

Office Furniture

Again, the choice is up to you. As a bare minimum, you will need a desk, a chair and a filing cabinet. Beyond that, select whatever furniture meets your needs, wants and budget.

THINGS YOU WILL NEED

Telephone

Although it can be done, using your home telephone line is not recommended. You should have a touch-tone line dedicated to business use. It is, however, a good idea to have two or three two-line telephone sets in addition to the one in your office. This will allow you to take business calls when you are in other parts of the house. If available, you should also have a call-waiting feature. Clients may be dissuaded by a busy signal.

A bonus of having additional two-line telephones is increased household peace. Having two telephone lines, each with call waiting, has allowed our two teenage daughters unlimited telephone time without our missing a call.

The best part is that your telephone line is tax deductible. When arranging your telephone service, make arrangements for a telephone credit card. This will enable you to charge long distance calls to your business number. Be sure to keep your card number confidential; anyone who has the number may make long distance calls and charge them to you.

Answering Machine

You should not try to operate your home business without one. Technological advances have resulted in very inexpensive and effective answering machines. Many telephones and fax machines now have them built in. The most useful features include voice activated message-taking, and remote access for picking up your calls and changing outgoing messages when away from the office.

Despite these technological conveniences, answering machines have limitations. The extent of information provided is often limited; the quality of the message received is often unintelligible. Further, many callers prefer to deal with humans.

Telephone Answering Service

I highly recommended this service. Incoming calls are forwarded to a telephone answering service where trained operators take your calls. Thus, you may enjoy two significant benefits. First, you will increase the number of messages you receive; some estimates indicate that live telephone answering results in at least 25% more messages than automated answering. Secondly, you present a professional and efficient image to callers. One individual who calls me on a regular basis comments on how busy my office sounds!

Computer

A computer is as essential to your home business as a telephone. It enables you to attend to client needs and administrative tasks without purchasing secretarial and clerical services.

The choice of computer is nearly limitless. The features that you select depend upon your needs and budget. If you are a "techno-peasant," select a supplier who is prepared to help you identify and meet your needs and not simply sell you the latest equipment available. The enthusiasm of computer salespeople often dazzles customers into purchasing more sophisticated equipment than is necessary.

When I started my home business, I was a total techno-klutz. Before even using the system, I had to take some basic courses to learn about computer operation and keyboarding — typing on the computer keyboard. These courses involved a small expenditure of time and money but were well worth the effort.

Computer Software

The viability of home businesses has increased in large part because of the availability of inexpensive and effective computer technology. Projects that formerly required sophisticated computer facilities in costly office premises may now be effectively and efficiently completed by home businesses. In addition to the broad range of affordable and readily available software, the following programs can assist you in the administration and management of your business.

Word processing. With appropriate word processing software, you need never again depend upon an assistant to complete your paper work. Regardless of the program you select, make sure that it has spell check and grammar check capabilities.

Spreadsheet. The calculations outlined in the next chapter are a breeze with a simple spreadsheet program. The versatility and usefulness of spreadsheet applications in home business operations are truly amazing. These uses include cash flow forecasting and simple data analysis.

Accounting.   Obviously, you are going to have to keep track of your revenues and expenses. Many accounting packages include cheque writing features and produce financial reports on a regular basis. If you have a computer, there is no reason for maintaining your financial records manually.

Contact/client data base.   This program will allow you to track all current and potential customers and contacts. Many also allow you to undertake mass mailings. For a very small initial investment, you will have a very powerful marketing tool.

Desktop publishing.   Unless you plan to produce a large volume of print communication, this is not essential. For newsletters and presentations, most word processing programs will provide adequate quality.

Printer

If your business will involve the preparation of reports and other written material, you should invest in a laser printer. Otherwise, a good quality dot matrix printer will prove adequate. As with all computer equipment, make the purchasing decision on the basis of what you need rather than what the sales representative has to sell.

Fax Machine

There are a number of variations on the basic fax machine. One is the standard model with a dedicated telephone line. Another is the combination of fax and answering machine. Newer models have a built-in silicone chip that distinguishes incoming calls as either fax or telephone and routes the call accordingly. This approach is very popular with home business operators. A third approach is to have a fax card installed in your computer and attached to a modem. This will enable you to use your computer terminal to send and receive fax messages. This technique works especially well if all the faxes you send are computer generated.

Yet another approach involves using a special service, "Ident-i-Call," offered by telephone companies. This involves having the telephone company assign two numbers, each with a different ring, to a single telephone line. One number would receive voice communications, the other fax transmissions. A "ring-identifier" recognizes the appropriate ring for faxes and sends the transmission to the fax machine.

Copier

There are many small and relatively inexpensive copiers designed for home use. The alternative to having a home copier is to make regular trips to quick print shops. You can also have copies made in many office supply stores, drug stores, libraries and so forth. If you are making a large number of copies of relatively few documents, it is least expensive and most convenient to have the copying done in a quick print shop.

Cellular Telephone

Unless you plan to make and receive a large number of telephone calls away from your office, a cellular phone is not absolutely essential. Before committing yourself, track the number of calls you make away from your office and record the accessibility of public phones.

If you do purchase a cellular telephone, select a totally portable model. This will enable you to carry the phone with you if you travel in a vehicle other than our own and allows you to use your phone even when away from any vehicles.

Pager

Unless it is important that your callers have instant access to you, a pager is not necessary. With an answering machine or an answering service, you check regularly for messages and keep in touch with your callers without the expense and sense of urgency that are features of pagers.

Line Manager

This is a device that fits onto your telephone line to direct incoming calls to their appropriate destinations: telephone, answering machine, fax or computer modem. This is a must if you use more than one piece of equipment connected to your telephone line.

Modem

If you exchange computer data with anyone else, you will require a modem — a device that enables you to plug into the information highway. If you use a computer modem, you must also have **and use** anti-virus software.

Specialized Equipment

If your business generates a great deal of mail, you will probably want a postage meter. If you will be collating and stapling many batches of printed material, you might need collating equipment and an electric stapler. Think carefully about your needs in this area.

Office Supplies

This includes everything from pens, pencils and paper to pins, tape and paper clips. You probably won't need very much of any one thing at first, so don't buy in large quantities until you know the volume that you will be using.

Stationery

Your paper wardrobe — stationery — is one of your most important marketing tools. Since it is unlikely that your client and potential clients will be seeing your office, your stationery must convey an image of competence and professionalism. The time and effort involved in designing good letterhead and business cards will be returned several times over. Invest the time and money necessary to get the best stationery you can afford. In selecting paper, you may consider recycled — excellent quality recycled paper stock is available.

Automobile

If you use your vehicle to travel from your place of business (your home) to your clients' places of business, related automobile expenses will be tax deductions. Unless you use your automobile exclusively for business, only a portion of automobile expenses will be tax deductible. Check with your accountant.

Licenses, Permits, etc.

As a rule, you do not need a license or permit to operate a business from your home. Some businesses such as hairdressing, and medical or dental services do require licensing. Make sure you know if you must have one. Check with your local municipal government.

Tax Registrations

If you will be collecting sales taxes from your customers you must register with the appropriate tax authorities. Check with your local tax offices to determine the registration procedure.

Membership Fees

These include fees for membership in professional and trade associations as well as business and local ones. Some membership fees qualify as deductible business expenses; check with your accountant about your particular situation.

Property Insurance

Although it is unlikely you will require special insurance for your home business, you should check with your agent or broker to insure that your current property insurance will cover your business assets. You might also ask whether you can purchase business interruption insurance. This covers the costs involved should the operation of your business be interrupted by major property damage to your home.

Liability Insurance

If it is available and reasonably priced and if there is any risk of your clients suffering a loss as to a result of your services, you might consider liability insurance. If liability insurance is either not available or too costly, you can limit your personal liability by incorporating your business.

Life Insurance

Although not likely to be considered a business expense, life insurance remains an important component of your business operation. Term insurance rather than whole life is probably best because it provides low-cost protection. The premiums can be paid by the business and charged back to you personally.

Disability Insurance

Like life insurance, this is not usually a business expense, although the premiums can be paid by the business and charged back to you. It is, however, important that you have adequate coverage to protect your income in the event of illness or disability.

Banking Services

Your banker can be your best friend as you start your own business. However, it is important that you select someone whom you like and who understands your business activities. Many entrepreneurs use different institutions for their business and personal finances. You will need some or all of the following services.

Chequing Account These come in many forms and are known by many names. Make sure you understand the features of the account you select including any service charges.

Line of Credit This is a form of loan designed to cover the period between completing work for your client and receiving the payment. Many a business has been saved by a line of credit. Again, make sure you understand the costs involved.

Credit Card Some banks and financial institutions offer credit cards issued under the business name; others will issue the cards only in your own name. The bewildering array of options make it difficult to make the most appropriate choice. Some form of credit card is, however, a must for business operations.

Other Today's institutions offer a broad range of other services to business clients. My bank, for example, offers a card that allows me to use automatic banking machines to access my business accounts. As with all financial activities, make sure you understand what you are getting and how much you are paying for it.

Accountant

With good accounting or bookkeeping software you may not need a book-keeper or accountant once you're up and running. Your system can prepare all the statements you need. You might, however, need an accountant to interpret the statements or provide you with tax advice and prepare your tax returns. If you decide you want an accountant, you don't necessarily need one with a professional designation such as Certified Public Accountant or Chartered Accountant. Many without such titles can provide you with the same quality of financial and tax advice at a much lower cost. As ever, make sure you understand what you are getting from your accountant and how much you will pay.

Lawyer

You can set up and run your business without necessarily involving a lawyer. However, there are times when you must consult one. These situations would include clarification as to the applicability to your business of specific laws, regulations or municipal bylaws, alleged violation of any statutes, and commencement or defence of court actions.

Shop around for the lawyer who will provide you with the services you need at a price you are willing to pay. Competition in the profession may make it possible for you to have an initial consultation with a lawyer at no charge.

Other

Obviously, no two home businesses are alike. Some people may start their businesses without any decorating or structural changes to their homes, while others may require renovations or additions. Some business people might need marketing help while others might require computer assistance. Before leaving the start-up checklist make sure you have added any special needs you might have.

10

FINANCIAL STATEMENTS

Financial statements are essential in planning and operating a home business. Forecasts provide a good indication of the revenue that must be produced to cover operating expenses. Statements prepared at regular intervals allow you to assess the financial health of your business and monitor your progress towards your goals. There are several types of financial statements, each used for a different purpose, depending upon the development stage of the business. The following material outlines those statements that are most likely to be necessary for a home business.

START-UP STATEMENT
As its name indicates, this statement shows the financial status of a business at its beginning.

Sources and Uses of Funds
This statement shows where the money is coming from to start your business (source) and what these funds are purchasing (uses).

This format can be easily adapted for spreadsheet use. Customize the statement by adding elements that apply to your business and deleting those that do not.

The following is a sample statement showing Source and Uses of Funds.

Source:

Owner's Equity _____

Loan _____

Total Funds from All Sources (A) _____

Uses:

Office Furniture _____

Office Equipment _____

Specialized Equipment _____

Office Supplies _____

Computer Software _____

Stationery _____

Automobile _____

Licenses, permits, etc. _____

Insurance _____

Legal, Accounting, Consulting _____

Total Use of Funds: (B) _____

Working Capital: (A-B) _____

Working capital is the amount of money available to operate the business.

FORECASTING STATEMENTS

These statements are attempts to forecast or predict the financial results of operating your business over the first few years. Like all attempts to forecast the future they are subject to many unknowns. They will, however, serve as indications of what you hope to achieve. They will also serve as budget guidelines to help control spending.

Cost of Goods Sold

If your business involves purchasing or manufacturing goods, it will be important to know the cost of these goods.

Following is a procedure for determining the cost of goods sold for a specific period of time, such as a month, quarter or year.

Inventory at beginning of period:

plus	Labor	_____
plus	Purchases	_____
	Sub-total	_____
less	Inventory at end	_____
	Total Cost of Goods Sold	_____

For the first forecasting statement, the dollar value of inventory would usually be 0; normally inventory is not acquired until the business has started. For subsequent statements, the dollar value of inventory at the beginning of one period is the same as the dollar value at the end of the preceding period.

Labor represents the cost of labor — yours and those people whom you pay to help produce inventory.

The cost of goods sold will also be a component of the income statement outlined following.

Operating Overhead

Projecting revenue for the first time is the most difficult aspect of financial forecasting.

Projections will be based on such factors as how much

is charged for units of goods and services and what volume of business is expected. Unless past experience makes it possible to estimate your fee revenue, the financial projections will be based on a limited amount of reliable information. In this case, the best approach is to work from what is known to what is not. Thus, before addressing revenue projections, which are difficult to determine the first time, it is best to first calculate monthly overhead amounts, which are easily identified, and then project the revenue needed to meet or exceed your overhead figures.

Typical Expenses

The following list details typical expense items. It is not likely that all of them will apply to any one business. Conversely, it is possible that many businesses will have expense items that are not included in this list. As with start-up expenses, customize this list to meet your own needs. Amounts for individual items can be based on estimates provided by suppliers, or estimated as a percentage of total expenses.

Expense Item	Monthly	Annual
Accounting/Legal		
Automobile		
Bank Charges		
Depreciation		
Dues/Subscriptions		
Employee Benefits		
Insurance		
Interest		

Licenses/Taxes _____ _____

Marketing/Sales Promo _____ _____

Miscellaneous _____ _____

Postage/Courier _____ _____

Printing/Copying _____ _____

Personal Development _____ _____

Rent _____ _____

Salaries/Wages _____ _____

Stationery/Office Supplies _____ _____

Telephone _____ _____

Utilities _____ _____

There are two approaches to recording these expenses.

The *Cash* approach involves recording the expenses when actually paid; the *Accrual* approach involves recording the expenses when incurred (or billed) regardless of when the expense is paid. Each approach has advantages and disadvantages. The cash approach is the simplest to maintain. Profit or loss for a given period may be determined by deducting all expenses paid for a period from all revenue received for the same period. It does, however, fail to consider accounts receivable — accounts sent to clients but not yet paid — and accounts payable — bills received but not yet paid. Accordingly, it doesn't represent a true picture of profitability.

Although more difficult to maintain, the accrual method presents a more accurate picture of profitability. Profit is determined by deducting all expenses incurred for the period, regardless of whether paid or not, from the value of all goods or services provided during the period. Since only sales revenue and expenses for a particular period are considered, the statement represents a more accurate indication of the profitability for that period.

Regardless of which approach is adopted, it should be followed consistently. The following form will assist you in determining your cash disbursements for the first 12-month period.

Typical Cash Disbursement Forecast for First 12-Month Period												
Month	**1**	**2**	**3**	**4**	**5**	**6**	**7**	**8**	**9**	**10**	**11**	**12**
Accounting and legal												
Clerical support[†]												
Dues and subscriptions												
Insurance												
Licenses and taxes												
Marketing												
Other												
Printing and copying												
Professional development												
Stationery and office supplies												
Telephone and postage												
Vehicle												
Total Disbursements												

† This would include secretarial and clerical services purchased from outside sources.

CASH FLOW FORECAST

As its name suggests, a cash flow forecast is a forecast of cash flowing into and out of a business. The forecast is based on predictions of when payment from clients is expected and when payments to suppliers and to yourself are expected.

Prepare your cash flow forecast using as much detail as you believe appropriate. And consider the following factors.

Revenue

- Regardless of the payment provisions on invoices, most customers will pay 30–60 days after they have been invoiced.
- Some customers, especially the government, will pay more than 60 days after invoice date.
- Some customers will not pay at all.
- Until your business credibility is well established, few customers will pay anything in advance.

Expenses

- Some suppliers will demand pre-payment.
- Most suppliers will demand payment in 30 days or less.

Cash Disbursements

These are to be recorded when actual payment is expected. For improved management information, each of the expense categories may be further classified into sub-categories.

Accounting and legal. Normally, accounting expenses are high around tax time. Barring unforeseen problems, legal expenses will be high only at start-up.

Clerical support. These expenses, usually low in slow times, will be higher when larger projects are anticipated.

Dues and subscriptions. Membership dues for professional and trade associations are usually paid annually; subscriptions may be paid at more frequent intervals. This category should be subdivided.

Insurance. Although insurance premiums are normally billed annually, many companies will provide interim or installment billing.

Licenses and taxes. These are usually paid on an installment basis.

Marketing

Other } Monthly averages can be used for

Printing and Copying these items.

Personal development. If you know when specific courses and training will be taken, the expense details can be recorded in the appropriate months.

Stationery and office supplies. Use monthly averages.

Telephone and postage. Use monthly averages.

Vehicle. Total projected operating expenses can be averaged over a 12-month period.

Personal Draw

This represents the compensation that you will receive for managing the business and delivering services to your clients. Personal draws should be taken on a regular basis. To ensure that the business maintains a strong cash flow, set the amount of the draw at a level that covers what is required for household and personal expenses. As the business begins to show a profit, you can pay yourself a bonus from any accumulated cash surplus.

Revenue

Obviously, if a business is to survive in the long run, revenue must at least equal overhead. Profit comes from the revenue that remains after the overhead has been paid.

In the absence of more reliable information, the best means of forecasting profit is to set a specific income goal. This should be determined after consideration of both past income and your personal financial needs.

Allowing two weeks holidays, weekends off and ten statutory holidays, there will be 240 working days per year. Dividing the income goal by 240 will determine your daily income goal. By combining this figure with the daily overhead amount as determined previously, you will have identified the amount of income that must be generated daily to achieve personal income goal and meet overhead.

The following form will assist in preparing a cash flow forecast. This form can be readily adapted to spreadsheet use. Completing a cash flow forecast is another exercise that is easier with the use of a computer spreadsheet. If you plan to complete the forecast manually, prepare a customized form modeled on the following forms. Modify them by adding your own descriptions of disbursements, cash receipts and revenues. Make a number of photocopies of the forms and complete them using a calculator, pencil and eraser. If nothing else, this exercise will demonstrate the need for spreadsheet software!

Typical Cash Flow Forecast for First 12-Month Period

Month	1	2	3	4	5	6	7	8	9	10	11	12
CASH RECEIPTS Fee Revenue												
Other Revenue												
TOTAL REVENUE												
TOTAL DISBURSEMENTS (from previous chart)												
NET CASH FLOW												
CUMULATIVE CASH FLOW												

If your business involves the sale of goods, ensure that the forecast includes provisions for the purchase of goods or materials from which goods will be produced.

You now have the necessary information to forecast revenue and expenses for the first year of operation.

Income (Profit and Loss) Forecast

Income or profit is what is left over after all expenses have been paid. Expressed in terms of a formula, it is:

$$P \text{ (profit)} = R \text{ (revenue)} - E \text{ (expenses)}$$

If the business provides services only, determine profit by simply deducting expenses from revenue. If expenses exceed revenue, a loss has been incurred.

If the business sells products, modify the formula by deducting cost of goods sold from revenue *before deducting expenses*. In this case, there are two components to calculating profit, shown by the following formula.

First, deduct the cost of goods sold (CGS) from the revenue (R). The procedure for calculating CGS is found earlier on page 85.

$$\text{G (gross) P (profit)} = \text{R} - \text{CGS}$$

The next step is to calculate the net profit (P) by deducting expenses (E) from the Gross Profit (GP).

$$P = GP - E$$

PROJECTED INCOME STATEMENTS

These project quarterly revenue over a period of one-two years. By summarizing the cash flow forecasts, they project the income that can be expected if the business develops as planned. The operating expenses can be classified into whatever categories are most useful and meaningful. The following form will assist in the preparation of these statements.

Projected Income Statement

	First Quarter	Second Quarter	Third Quarter	Fourth Quarter	Total Year 1	Total Year 2
Fee Revenue						
Less: Expenses Operating						
Marketing						
Other						
Operating Profit						
Less: Your Draw						
Net Income						

ON-GOING STATEMENTS

After a business has been operating for some time, a number of financial statements are needed to measure the financial health of the business.

Balance Sheet

This statement is like a snapshot taken at a specific point in time. It records the dollar value of assets such as inventory, accounts receivable, furniture, fixtures and automobiles. It also lists debts and other liabilities such as accounts payable and loans payable. One section of the statement — owner's equity — refers to the value of the owners' interest in the business. This amount is calculated by deducting the total liabilities from the total assets. As a result, the formula on which a balance sheet is based is as follows:

$$\text{A (assets)} - \text{L (liabilities)} = \text{E (equity)}$$

Income (Profit and Loss) statement

Like its forecast cousin, this statement provides a summary of profits or losses realized over a period of time — a month, a quarter, or a year. Unlike the forecast, the statement is historical — it reflects what actually happened.

As your business grows and develops the financial statements will become increasingly detailed and sophisticated. However, most will be based on the statement formats discussed above.

Maintaining proper financial records is a crucial element of operating a business. Effectively interpreting these statements is a key management responsibility. Fortunately, there are innumerable publications, training courses, software and other tools to help clarify the various aspects of this area. Look for bookkeeping and accounting help in book stores, public libraries, educational organizations and professional accounting associations. Any or all of these sources can help simplify what might otherwise be an overwhelming and tedious chore.

11

YOUR BUSINESS PLAN

Unless you enjoy the challenge of discovering new territories without any kind of assistance, you are not likely to try to reach an unfamiliar destination without a road map. Using a map helps minimize the risks of getting lost.

Similarly, by using a business plan you can minimize the risks of losing time and money usually associated with starting a new business venture. Uniform road maps are readily available from a wide variety of sources. Business plans, on the other hand, are neither uniform nor readily available. You must prepare your own plan, reflecting your unique characteristics and those of your business. In preparing your plan, you should be as specific as possible to provide a sense of direction for the coming year. You must also provide enough flexibility to enable you to respond to new and unexpected opportunities as they arise.

As well as providing you with the requisite sense of direction, a well-prepared business plan will assist you in dealings with your bankers and other sources of financing.

DEVELOPING YOUR PLAN

The following material outlines details that are usually found in business plans. Consider only those elements that are relevant to your specific business. If there are issues relevant to your business that are not addressed, incorporate your consideration of these issues into your own plan.

Objectives

Your objectives will describe in detail the products or services that you will provide. They could reflect the image you want to project to your clients. They might also reflect the market or niche market in which you plan to specialize, and the type of client base you would like to build. In their finished form, your objectives should read like the copy for a well-prepared 30-second commercial: clean, concise and complete.

Competition

A thorough analysis of your competition is essential. This will include answers to the following questions:
- Who are your competitors?
- Where are they located?
- How long have they been in business?
- How do they price their services?
- Who are their major customers?
- What are their unique strengths?
- What are their unique weaknesses?
- What can they do better than I can?
- What can I do better than they can?

Gather the information necessary for this analysis from your own knowledge of the competition, from suppliers,

clients, colleagues, third parties or anyone with solid information about your competition.

When reviewing information, consider its source. Is the
information realistic and believable? Is the source of the
information credible? Is the information intended to be
deceptive or to mislead? Once you have analyzed the information, develop a profile of the competition that will make
it possible to differentiate your business from theirs. The
profile will also make it possible to project why clients will
prefer your services over those of the competition. A written
summary of the analysis will form part of the business plan.

Clients
For purposes of the business plan, prepare a brief summary
describing your clients and the needs they have that you
will be meeting. (Defining your client base is addressed in
detail in the following chapter.)

Pricing Your Services
Include a brief summary covering:
- Hourly and daily rate.
- Average fees per project.
- Projected total fees.
- Break-even point — level of sales to just cover operating
  expenses.
- Comparison of your prices to the competition.

Again, use only those items that apply to your business —
if you supply products, only the last three items would be
included.

Operating Requirements
This section of the business plan identifies the licenses, permits

and resources that you will require to begin and maintain your operation. Included in these requirements are:

- Compliance with federal, provincial or state and municipal government regulations.
- Obtaining the necessary permits and licenses to conduct your specific business.
- Registration for the collection of sales tax, if applicable.
- Acquisition of major pieces of equipment and furniture.
- Skills required to provide services to clients, and the source and cost of acquiring those skills.
- If dealing with third-party financing, i.e., banks or private investors, an outline of your own relevant skills and experience to confirm that you can make a success of your business.

Financial Considerations: Start-up and Forecasting Statements.

The preceding chapter outlines how to prepare these statements. In their final form, they should be incorporated into the business plan.

Using Your Plan

Once prepared, your business plan should not be consigned to the bottom drawer of your desk. Just as you use a road map to monitor your progress toward a destination, you should use your plan to monitor progress towards your ultimate business goals. If the business is developing as planned, you can be confident that, if you stay the course, you will achieve your overall goals. Conversely, if things are not developing as planned, you can make mid-course corrections or modify your goals. Your business plan can and will serve as an effective road map, provided you consult it regularly.

12

HOW TO
MARKET YOUR
HOME BUSINESS

The concept of marketing is relatively new to the business world. It arose in the 1950s to challenge the approaches that manufacturers followed in getting their goods into the hands of the end consumer.

One such approach — *the production concept* — holds that consumers will favor products that are widely available and low in cost. Managers of production-oriented organizations concentrate on achieving high production efficiency and wide distribution coverage. Ford Motor Company, for example, puts much of its resources into perfecting the mass production of standardized automobiles to bring down their costs so that ordinary consumers can afford them. For many modern consumers, standardization is no longer desirable. They look for products and services that meet their own unique needs.

Another marketing approach — *the product concept* — holds that consumers will favor those products that offer the most quality, performance and features. Managers in these product-oriented organizations focus on making good products and improving them over time. This concept exemplifies the cliché: build a better mousetrap and the world will beat a path to your door. However, experience has taught us that this is not always true. Just because you may have a better mousetrap doesn't mean that it will sell. What makes it better than the others? How will the world know about your product or that it is better than the rest? How will the world know where to find the mousetrap? And does the world really need another mousetrap? These are just a few of the questions that challenge the validity of the product concept.

A third approach — *the selling or sales concept* — holds that consumers, if left alone, will ordinarily not buy enough of a given organization's products. The organization must undertake aggressive selling and promotion effort. Selling is often supported by extensive advertising and promotional campaigns. Often, closing the sale becomes more important than the product or service and the customer. As a result, many consumers confuse marketing with advertising and hard selling.

Peter Drucker, a leading management expert, commented:

> There will always, one can assume, be need for some selling. But the aim of marketing is to make selling superfluous. *The aim of marketing is to know and understand the customer so well that the product or service fits him and sells itself* [emphasis added]. Ideally, marketing should result in a customer who is ready to buy. All that should be needed then is to make the product or service available.[13]

The *marketing concept* stresses that the key to achieving your business goals consists of determining the needs and expectations of your clients and meeting them more effectively and efficiently than your competitors.

Non-technical ways of expressing this approach include: "Find needs and fill them" and "make what will sell, don't try to sell what you can make."

Based on this approach, we may define *marketing* as *the process of identifying your clients' needs and expectations and using your resources to meet these needs and expectations.*

THE FUNCTION OF MARKETING

Marketing has two very important purposes.

First and foremost, *it helps to protect and maintain your current client base.* Increasing competition in today's marketplace means that your clients are probably targets for others. For your business to continue to thrive in the long term, you must protect your client base from your competition. This can best be done by insuring that you continue to meet your clients' needs on an on-going basis. Defensive marketing activities — maintaining regular contact with your customers, understanding their changing needs and demonstrating your responsiveness — will help protect your client base from erosion.

It is more efficient and profitable to provide services to existing clients than to court new ones. Less time is required to develop an understanding of the client and his or her needs; past dealings provide a wealth of useful information.

Secondly, *marketing activities generate new customers.* This new business consists of providing existing services to new clients. You are already able to deliver the service effectively and efficiently; only the clients are new.

An alternate source of new business would be to

provide new services to new clients. Because these clients are new, you must identify their needs, wants and expectations.

You cannot rely on existing relationships; you must establish your credibility and credentials with each new client *before* you can promote your new services.

There are two challenges — selling yourself and selling your service — to be met before the sale can be closed. Clearly, trying to sell new services to new clients is the most difficult approach to obtaining new business.

DEVELOPING YOUR MARKETING PLAN

Few marketing activities are likely to generate significant new business in the short term. Effective marketing involves the use of many strategies over a period of time. Because of this, a marketing plan is essential. It identifies your clients and their needs, clarifies your overall marketing goals and defines specific strategies. The following steps outline the development of your marketing plan.

1. **Identify your clients and their needs.**
    *   Who are your current and potential clients?
    *   What do they do? What business are they in?
    *   What is their sales volume? How many people do they employ? What fee will you receive from providing them with services?
    *   Where are they located?
    *   What do they need from you today? What will they need from you in the future? What do they *expect* from you today? Will they expect the same things in the future? If not, what will they expect?

Don't guess at the answers to questions addressing clients' needs. If you don't know the answers, find out by asking your clients directly. If you have already done work for them, the best means of identifying their future needs is by combining a client satisfaction interview, as outlined in Chapter 14, with some form of needs assessment. This assessment would focus on the trends that the clients recognize in their own industry and how those trends will affect their operation. As you discuss the impact of these trends, you may also talk about which services your clients anticipate requiring from you.

It may be necessary to do some secondary research in reference libraries or by asking others familiar with the client. Your network contacts identified in Chapter 15 can also be of immeasurable benefit.

2. **Match your resources to your clients' needs.**
   - What can you do *now* to meet your clients' needs?
   - What additional resources — people, money, equipment, skills — do you require now? In the future?
   - What can you do better, faster, cheaper than your competition? How can you do this?
   - What additional resources — people, money, equipment skills — do you require to maintain your competitive edge?

Be brutally honest with yourself in completing this assessment. You should identify your strengths and weaknesses and those of your competition to be sure that you are in fact the best person to serve your current and potential clients. You should take steps to correct any weaknesses or improve any areas in which your competition is surpassing you.

3. **Marketing communications.**
    *   How can you tell your current and target clients that you can meet their needs better, faster, cheaper than your competition? How frequently will you have to do this?

Communications could include meetings and interviews, speeches and formal presentations, personal letters and personalized mailings, newsletters, brochures, specialized hand-out material and advertising. Regardless of which communication tool you use, be sure that it is the most appropriate vehicle for the people with whom you wish to communicate.

4. **Putting it all together.**
    *   Define your current and target customers.
    *   Define current services and those you plan to deliver to each.
    *   Determine how you will acquire the necessary skills to deliver new services.
    *   Identify how you will communicate with current and potential clients.
    *   Develop a time frame and budget for marketing communications.

Once your plan has been prepared, it will serve as a blueprint as you market your services. The plan should be fairly general and flexible so that you can respond to new opportunities. Plans that are too rigid tend to be more of a handicap than a useful tool; they may interfere with effective marketing and become obstacles to your success.

13

MARKETING STRATEGIES

To achieve your marketing goals, you must identify and follow appropriate marketing strategies. These will help you keep in touch with current clients and identify potential ones, while telling them about your product or service. Marketing strategies in and of themselves are unlikely to bring new business to you. They will, however, help set up the opportunity to generate new business.

These strategies fall into one of two categories: *personal contact* and *planned communication*. In the final analysis, it is your ability to sell both yourself and your services that will generate new business. To do this, you must deal with your current and target clients on a personal basis.

PERSONAL CONTACT

The purpose of this contact is to establish and maintain personal relationships with a broad range of individuals. The most commonly used methods are *networking* (discussed in greater detail in Chapter 16) and *participation in clubs and organizations*.

Networking

This is the practice of establishing and maintaining personal contact with a broad range of individuals — including current and potential clients, referral sources, information sources and "bird dogs," who may point you in the direction of potential clients. Networking is one of the most effective marketing techniques because it has many long-term benefits. Properly practised, it is possible to enhance personal relationships with existing clients as well as develop new relationships with potential ones. Regular contact with members of your network enables you to monitor and respond effectively to new developments affecting your customers.

> **Advantages.**   Provided it is backed up by excellent services, networking helps build a third party sales force — contacts who promote your services and make referrals to you. As a result, it provides ongoing round-the-clock marketing. Your personal credibility with your network contacts is vital in providing a strong foundation for marketing and cross-selling additional services. Ideally, it is a subtle approach — you can sell yourself without being perceived as though you're selling. As your network contacts promote you to their own contacts, you may extend your reach and image far beyond your immediate circle of friends and acquaintances.
>
> **Disadvantages.**   Effective networking is not necessarily easy. It requires discipline, an outgoing personality and a solid understanding of the selling process. It is also very time-consuming. Fortunately, there is

excellent contact management software available to help with the logistics of maintaining contact with your personal network. Results are seldom instantaneous; it is common for network contacts to generate new business months and even years after the initial contact was made.

Membership in Clubs and Organizations

Joining sports, social, community and charitable organizations may provide you with opportunities to meet potential clients. However, your participation will not be effective if you join for business purposes only; other members may see your participation as a sham and be reluctant to either do business with you or take you seriously as a member of the organization. You must be committed to the goals of the organization and enjoy participation for its own sake.

Advantages. Provided you are committed to the organization, your participation can be rewarding, as well as serving to increase your personal profile and enabling you to make contact with possible clients and potentially influential individuals. Once the initial contact has been made, you can add these people to your personal network for future follow-up.

Disadvantages. The primary purpose of your participation in an organization should not be to further your marketing. You should also want to meet personal needs or serve your community. The organization's activities should, in general, take precedence over your marketing activities.

PLANNED COMMUNICATIONS

The aim here should be to present clear messages about yourself, your credentials and your ability to assist clients. These messages are directed to specifically identified individuals or groups of individuals and should be carefully planned and structured.

Formal Presentations

Prepared speeches and presentations to specifically identified groups are ideal opportunities to demonstrate your knowledge of a particular subject, confirm your expertise in existing areas and to introduce new products or services. These events may increase your profile and enhance your image.

There are many types of presentations including speeches, seminars and workshops. All can be very effective. The type you use depends upon your own personal style and comfort level in front of a group of people. The content of your message, the size, needs and interests of the audience as well as the occasion also influence the type of presentation. Your approach can be hard or soft sell, serious or amusing. If it is to have long term-benefits, a presentation must be both credible and memorable.

In preparation for any kind of presentation, it is very important to learn as much as possible about the audience. How many people will there be? Who are they? Why will they be listening to your presentation? Knowing your audience and their level of understanding of your subject matter will allow you to table your presentation to meet their needs and to conduct appropriate follow-up.

It is also important to develop your own oral presentation skills. Your voice, your manner and body language and your ability to express ideas clearly as well as being sensitive to your audience are at least as important as the content of your presentation. These skills may be honed through courses, individual consultation, coaching and practice. Preparation and follow-up generally take much longer than the presentation itself.

Speeches and demonstrations. These are essentially one-way communications. The presenter speaks and demonstrates and the audience listens and watches. Charts, samples or audio-visual materials may be used. There may be opportunities for audience questions at the end, but the communication is mainly one way.

Seminars and workshops. These involve more interaction between the presenter and audience — often relatively few in number. The interactive format enables you to exchange information with members of the audience, and for them to exchange information with each other. This format enables you to meet individual participants if only briefly. Again, follow-up is important to ensure long-term benefits to you and to the audience members.

As well as good oral communication skills, effective group leadership skills are essential. Audience members will respond positively if they feel they have made a contribution to the discussion and will take some useful information away with them.

In all forms of presentation, learn the art of brevity. Know what the time limits are and respect them even if you must omit part of your material. Start and end on time. Leave your audience wanting more.

Print Communications

Included in this category are brochures, circulars, flyers, and similar printed material prepared for either general distribution or a specific audience or occasion. Attractive and informative materials can effectively communicate unique features of your business to existing and potential customers and network contacts. Distributed as part of a presentation to an audience, print material reinforces your spoken message and serves as a reminder of you and your presentation.

With appropriate computer equipment you can produce some kinds of print materials yourself. However, bear in mind that the quality of your printed materials will reflect the quality of your business. The materials should be attractive, easy to read and error-free. This is an area in which critical feedback from others is essential — it is also a good opportunity to involve others in your business as suggested in Chapter 15. Depending on the nature of your business and the extent of your own talents, you may decide to budget for professional design and printing.

Benefits can be long-term if the material is attractive, interesting or useful enough to be saved for future reference. Material should be kept current and distributed continuously. Bear in mind, however, that even the best printed materials are not substitutes for personal involvement with existing or potential clients.

Advertising

This is paid promotion of your business. Because you control the message, advertising is potentially very effective;

you can reach a large audience. However, advertising will be effective only for generating new leads. It can stimulate interest in your product or service; it is not likely to close the sale.

The wide range of available advertising media, including print and electronic media, billboards and transit advertising, enables you to select the appropriate advertising vehicle to reach your target audience. This can be very costly. Remember that your message will have a great deal of competition. We are all exposed to thousands of commercials every day, most of which are ignored or quickly forgotten. In order to yield real benefits, your message must be directed at your identified target market. It might be advantageous to purchase the expertise of others to ensure effectiveness.

Direct Mail

This approach involves mailing specific information to individually-identified contacts. Newsletters are currently a popular form of direct mail. This technique is a very effective means of communicating with potential clients and of keeping in touch with your network contacts, existing clients and referral sources.

For best results, avoid using mailing labels. Instead, print directly onto envelopes. Studies have shown that the use of postage stamps rather than postage meters increases the effectiveness of the mailing. Individuals who receive what appears to be personally addressed and stamped mail tend to be curious about the contents and are more likely to open the envelope and read your communication.

Direct mail is relatively low in cost, especially when using versatile computer programs that ensure properly targeted mailings and effective follow-up. Mailings can be customized for each type of contact, current or potential client.

Direct mailings are obvious selling tactics and are often considered "junk mail." Further, your mailings must compete with countless others. Regardless of how carefully it is done, direct mail results in a very low response rate: you can consider your mailing successful if you realize a mere 1% return rate.

Writing for Publication

This approach increases your personal profile and professional credibility by demonstrating your specialized knowledge and expertise. It includes preparing articles for publication in journals, magazines, newsletters and newspapers published by others. Writing books for publication by others or yourself may also be included.

Writing provides useful information, and may maintain a long-lasting presence in the minds of your readers. Reprints of your writing can be used as additional marketing tools.

Needless to say, good writing requires a considerable time commitment. It includes planning, research and long hours in front of your word processor. Writing requires a combination of artistry, hard work and self-discipline. It can be highly rewarding from a personal as well as business point of view, but it is not for everyone! Getting your work published and sold is a major task in itself. It is usually difficult to have material published by others and self-publishing is a very complex, time-consuming and expensive process.

Public Relations

Public relations involves using the media to generate free publicity for you and your business. It is not advertising in that you do not pay for public exposure and endorsement. Good public relations is probably the best marketing technique available.

Comments by third parties, especially in the media, are thought to be more objective and hence more credible than tooting your own horn or paying someone else to do it. Because the third parties are not usually paid to endorse, pubic relations can be inexpensive.

It takes considerable time and effort on your part to attract the attention of media people — editors, reporters, writers or columnists. Your information must be newsworthy and interesting to readers. It must compete for space with many other equally interesting materials.

14

MEASURING CLIENT SATISFACTION

Client satisfaction can be measured using a number of methods. Table 14-1 outlines different approaches that might be used.

TABLE 14–1

Methods of Measuring Client Satisfaction

Informal	Formal
Ask client contact	Interview client contact
Ask client employees	Interview client contact and decision makers
Ask client's other advisors e.g., lawyer, accountant	Evaluation on completion of work as in Table 14–2
Ask client's customers or clients	Client satisfaction survey as in Tables 14–3 and 14–4

INFORMAL TECHNIQUES

This approach involves simply checking on the client's satisfaction at appropriate stages. Anyone involved in the work may be asked for feedback. Table 14-1 lists typical individuals who might be asked for feedback. Use the following guidelines:

Be Very Selective When Asking for Feedback

Asking too often or of too many people suggests insecurity or lack of confidence. It is better to ask for feedback too seldom than too frequently.

Make clear that your request for feedback pertains to your services only. Soliciting feedback for the purpose of gathering additional information about your clients' activities could seriously jeopardize your relationship.

Obtain your client's approval before speaking to other employees, advisors or customers. Provided your request is framed in terms of "I would like to speak to ___ about the effectiveness of my services and how they may be improved," your client will probably approve of your plans. Otherwise, he or she may believes that you're trying to work behind his or her back.

Ensure that your request is specific and focused. A vague question like, "How am I doing?" will no doubt be answered with an equally vague, "Not too bad." Use the questions contained in Table 14-2 to frame your questions.

You could also ask the following questions:

- What am I doing that I should continue to do?
- What am I doing that I should stop doing?
- What am I not doing that I should start doing?

This will enable you to focus on specific issues and make whatever changes you and your client believe appropriate.

On receiving feedback, limit changes or modifications to

those necessary to ensure the client's immediate satisfaction. Unless absolutely essential, do not attempt a major overhaul as a mid-course correction. There is a significant difference between using client feedback to satisfy an individual client and using it to plan overall improvements. It is only after the immediate needs of clients have been attended to that consideration can be given to changes in practices and policies.

Valuable as it is, the informal approach to measuring client satisfaction has limitations. Like a single snapshot, it provides a view pertaining to one matter at a specific point in time. It does not indicate whether the satisfaction has increased or decreased over time; unless the client is specifically asked, there will be no identification of opportunities for improvement.

FORMAL TECHNIQUES

It is usually most effective to measure client satisfaction through a more formal structured approach. One such format involves interviews between you and representatives of your client. The material contained in Table 14-2 could be used in an interview. These interviews, conducted either by telephone or in person, can address a wide range of topics. They allow direct interaction between you and your clients, as well as providing your clients with the opportunity to expand on specific answers and provide additional information. A further advantage is that they often enable you to identify unmet client needs. Having recognized these needs, you are well positioned to demonstrate to the client just how well you can help meet them.

The interview process is, however, extremely time-consuming, and may be difficult to schedule.

The most cost-effective means of measuring client satisfaction is a formal survey conducted at fixed times. An ideal time to measure client satisfaction is immediately after you have completed the work. Another would involve significant dates for clients, such as fiscal year-ends or completion of routine reports. Table 14-2 is a sample of a client satisfaction questionnaire.

Each of the questions is designed to elicit specific feedback. The first question identifies specific services you provided to the client.

Question 2 identifies why the client selected you. This information is helpful in planning future marketing activities. Questions 3 and 4 measure the level of satisfaction with telephone contact. Questions 5 through 7 are intended to measure the client's overall satisfaction with your service. If completed, question 9 will enable you to try to undertake damage control with unhappy clients. Try to investigate any concerns and follow-up with the individual. This may enable you to prevent a similar problem in the future. You can also assure the client that his or her opinions are important to you.

The best format for questionnaires is a single, letter-sized form, printed on one side only. Such a questionnaire is more likely to be completed and returned than a longer one. You should send a covering letter, thanking the client for having chosen your firm, explaining the reason for the questionnaire, and requesting that the questionnaire be completed and returned as soon as possible. To increase the response rate, the questionnaire should be a separate mailing, that is, should not be included with another mailing. It should also include a self-addressed stamped or postage-paid envelope. If you have advertising specialties such as pens, pencils or key chains with your name on them, you

TABLE 14–2

How Did I Do?

For use on completion of work

I am committed to constantly improving the quality of my services to customers. Feedback is an important component of this process.

I would appreciate you taking a few minutes to complete this brief questionnaire. Please feel free to add comments.

1. Services provided _____

2. Why did you select my firm?
     previous or current client   _____
     referral from previous or current client   _____
     personal relationship   _____
     reputation   _____
     referral from _____
     advertising _____
     other _____

3. When you called my office, was the telephone answered to your
     satisfaction?   yes _____   no _____
     comments _____

4. Were your telephone calls returned within 24 hours?
                  yes _____   no _____

5. How satisfied are you with how the services were handled?

1	2	3	4	5
I —————— I —————— I —————— I —————— I

     very   satisfied   very
   satisfied   unsatisfied

     If unsatisfied, how could it have been handled better?

     _____

6. How could the overall quality of the services be improved?

     _____

7. Would you recommend the firm to others?
                  yes _____   no _____

8. Other comments (optional) _____

9. Name (optional) _____

should include one for your client as a thank you for his or her co-operation in the survey.

Except for the comments, which invite open-ended responses, the questionnaire lends itself to computer-assisted analysis.

As well as measuring satisfaction on completion of specific work, it is helpful to conduct general client satisfaction surveys from time to time. These should include satisfied as well as less-than-satisfied clients. To ensure a representative sample, respondents should be selected at random from the following groups to avoid bias:

- Type of client: individual, institutional, etc.
- Size of client, by sales or employees
- Clients from different practice areas
- Frequent and less frequent users
- Clients from different time periods.

It is important that questionnaire respondents include individuals who make the decisions as well as your client contacts. Ultimately, the decision makers are the individuals who must be satisfied; it is hoped that their satisfaction is based on the positive feedback of the actual answers.

Provided the sample is truly representative of your overall client base, the results of the survey should reflect your total client base.

Table 14-3 is a sample of a questionnaire that could be adapted for use in measuring the general satisfaction of individual clients.

Questions 3 through 6 are intended to measure clients' overall satisfaction with the firm's service. Similarly, if completed, question 9 will enable you to undertake damage control activities if necessary.

TABLE 14–3
Client Service Questionnaire
(For individuals)

I am committed to constantly improving the quality of my services to clients. Feedback is an important component of this process.

I would appreciate you taking a few minutes to complete this brief questionnaire. Please feel free to add comments.

1. Professional services provided _____

2. When you call my office, is the telephone answered to your satisfaction?   yes _____   no _____
comments _____

3. Are your telephone calls returned within 24 hours?
                yes _____   no _____
comments _____

4. How satisfied are you with how the services were handled?

1	2	3	4	5
I ——————— I ——————— I ——————— I ——————— I

very
satisfied   satisfied   very
                                                                    unsatisfied

If unsatisfied, how could it have been handled better?

_____

5. Please rate the overall quality of the services.

Excellent   _____   Very good   _____
Good   _____   Fair   _____
Poor   _____

6. How could the overall quality of the services be improved?

_____

7. Would you recommend our firm to others?
                yes _____   no _____
If so, why? _____
If not, why not? _____

8. Other comments (optional) _____

9. Name (optional) _____

TABLE 14–4
Quality Service Questionnaire
(For business clients)

	strongly agree				strongly disagree
1. You provide the level of services we expect.	1	2	3	4	5
comments or suggestions for improvements:					
2. You keep us informed of business and regulatory changes on a timely and proactive basis.	1	2	3	4	5
comments or suggestions for improvements:					
3. Your firm understands our business and the industry in which we operate.	1	2	3	4	5
comments or suggestions for improvements:					
4. You add value to our business by providing general business advice.	1	2	3	4	5
comments or suggestions for improvements:					
5. You complete various assignments on a timely basis, meet agreed upon deadlines and respond quickly to questions and other requests.	1	2	3	4	5
comments or suggestions for improvements:					
6. You return phone calls promptly.	1	2	3	4	5
comments or suggestions for improvements:					
7. You take an innovative and aggressive approach to resolving our business problems.	1	2	3	4	5
comments or suggestions for improvements:					

Table 14-4 is a sample questionnaire that could be used for conducting a quality service survey of business clients. This format could be adapted for government and institutional clients.

The format used in this sample will facilitate quick and easy responses by appropriate representatives of business or similar clients. This format also facilitates computer-assisted tabulation of the questionnaires.

IMPROVING CLIENT SATISFACTION

Client feedback is the starting point for improving satisfaction. Reassuring as it may be to learn that individuals are generally satisfied with your service, the real purpose of the surveys is to identify opportunities for *improving* client service.

Improvement opportunities can be identified in a number of ways. Individual comments can identify specific concerns. These might be isolated examples of problems in the delivery of service. If further investigation indicates that a problem exists, you should take remedial action to resolve the problem.

Individual concerns could also be early indications of a growing pattern. If this is the case, corrective action should be taken immediately.

Implementing improvements suggested by a survey can also provide you with a vehicle for obtaining additional feedback from clients. Once improvements have been defined but not yet implemented, individuals may be asked for their opinions.

For example, a client survey might indicate that a process by which information is exchanged between the firm and its clients could be improved. As a result, you have considered a number of alternative improvements, which may include the increased use of fax transmissions, the use of computer modems and the exchange of information on floppy disks. You might ask a number of clients which alternative they prefer. This could be done by asking them individually — in person, by phone or mail.

The measuring process provides an invaluable "feedback loop" for clients. It is this loop that provides clients with the opportunity of helping you to design and deliver services that meet their unique needs and expectations.

15

YOU ARE
NOT ALONE

Attractive as the idea may be, operating a business from your home involves some major challenges. One such challenge is integrating your business life with your personal life.

INTEGRATING YOUR FAMILY AND HOME BUSINESS

For many of us, our jobs are a central focus of our lives. Our education and training are intended to make us productive and contributing members of society. There is much rejoicing when we obtain our first real jobs, as opposed to temporary or part-time ones. Promotions are greeted with similar celebrations. Conversely, there is much despair if we lose our jobs. For many, the loss of a job is a form of death, with friends and relatives offering support. Our jobs give us a place to go, something to do, and colleagues with whom we may also socialize. This changes with the establishment of a home business.

Clearly, operating a home business requires adjustments to domestic life. If family members are expected to take the place of colleagues for purposes of discussing working and other current affairs, this expectation should be realistic. If you and your spouse do not share the same interest in baseball or politics, you might look elsewhere for a discussion partner. Similarly, if as work-at-home spouse, you are expected to undertake family chores, like starting meals or scheduling appointments, these expectations should be discussed and agreed upon.

Other areas in which family life and work life must each be adjusted include involvement of family members in the business, general housekeeping around designated office space, personal use of business equipment such as computer and telephone by family members and entertaining guests during business hours. All these issues may be easily resolved. The resolution does, however, require ongoing discussion and learning from experience.

Fighting Isolation

One reality of home business is that you will be working alone for considerable periods of time. You may not have colleagues and associates readily available to discuss work-related issues, help with decision making or even go for coffee to discuss the latest sports or political events. Running a business from home can be very lonely.

This sense of loneliness can also be experienced as you provide services to your clients. Although you may have chosen to limit your services to a narrow range, situations invariably arise in which your clients look to you for more services than you can realistically deliver. You may know what has to be done but lack the personal know-how and the network contacts to provide these additional services.

Administrative and management concerns can also seem overwhelming, especially if you lack relevant experience. Bookkeeping, mass mailings and a broad range of similar tasks can appear insurmountable obstacles for one individual operating a home business.

However, you need not work alone or in total isolation unless you choose to; there are ways of exchanging ideas and resources with others. Work gets done because people know and help others. In business, as in other areas of life, it is usually necessary to ask for what you need. The following groups of individuals outline possible sources of help.

Include Family, Friends and Neighbors

Remember that your family includes your immediate family — spouse and children — and your extended family — parents, siblings, aunts, uncles, cousins and so on. Your immediate family should be your primary source of moral and emotional support as you develop your business. They are the ones who will help you over the crises, large and small, that you may encounter. They will cheer your achievements and rejoice in your ultimate success. They can also provide invaluable assistance in all aspects of your business. My wife, for example has played a very active role in the development of this book.

Your extended family will know people you don't. This means that they might be able to refer you to specific resources — money, skills, expertise and knowledge — that you might not have otherwise known about.

Friends and neighbors can play a similar but more objective role. They too can provide moral support when you sense you have the entire weight of the world resting on your shoulders. They may also be able to refer you to resources that you might need.

INVOLVING FORMER COLLEAGUES AND ASSOCIATES

As most large organizations continue to cut back and downsize, many of your former colleagues and associates are doing the same thing you are; running their own business from home. This means that many of the services that were formerly available only from large organizations at a high cost are now readily accessible to you at affordable rates. This represents a growing source of client service and management help for you.

Your newly-independent former colleagues and associates can help you in three major ways. First, for a pre-arranged referral fee, you can refer work directly to these people, extending the range of services that you provide to your clients. Secondly, former associates may work with you in serving your clients, with their fees incorporated into your account. This will also extend your range of services. Thirdly, if they are unable to assist you directly, they may be able to refer you to others who can.

Don't be prepared to write off your former colleagues and associates who are still working with larger organizations. They and their business organization might be hungry for work. As a result, they might be very receptive to helping you serve your client for reduced fees. You won't know if you don't ask. Further, since they may be concerned about their own future with the organization, they may maintain contact with others like you who have started their own home business. This enables them to refer you to others who might have the resources you require. And just as these individuals can help you, you should be prepared to assist them in any way you can. This will help to increase the effectiveness of your referral network.

JOINING PROFESSIONAL, TRADE AND
BUSINESS ASSOCIATIONS

There are thousands of professional, trade and business associations in North America. These organizations exist for one or two main reasons: to promote the interests of their members; and to provide services to their members. Services could include training and continuing education, publications and networking opportunities.

To extend your network contacts, you should join one or more of those associations, preferably those whose members provide services similar to yours. This will provide access to a broad range of resources that will help you serve your clients better.

Thee are also many organizations that provide services to home businesses. Membership will help you operate your own business more effectively. Chapter 18 contains a partial listing of such associations. (If you know of any organization that is not listed but should be, please let me know so that I can add their names to future editions.)

DRAWING ON SUPPLIERS' RESOURCES

If asked, your suppliers can help you tremendously. Your suppliers include all those people who provide you with goods and services: your accountant, lawyer and banker, your marketing and advertising consultants, your office outfitter, your printer and so on. As well as providing you with specific goods and services they can provide such information as insights into how other businesses like yours have handled specific issues, details of new developments or new service opportunities that might be worth considering. Being active in the business community, they will also be in a position to refer you to potential clients and vice versa.

There are many other "hidden" suppliers who have great potential to help you. These include people whom you may not even know. They could include the neighbor down the street who used to be the bookkeeper in a large business and would now like to do some bookkeeping from her home. What about the former secretary who would like to do some word processing or similar work at home using her own computer or word processor? When I was having trouble with a new printer, I asked for help from a neighbor, whom I knew to be an engineer and very interested in computers. Not only was my problem resolved quickly, we reinforced the good neighbor policy on our street. With their high level of computer literacy many students make excellent part-time employees. There is considerable help available from these and similar "hidden" suppliers. All you have to do is to discover it and ask for it. You may be pleasantly surprised at the results.

These suggestions include only some of the possible sources of help as you develop and operate your home business. Your own resources and contacts can extend this list considerably. In seeking outside help, remember that help is available — you just have to ask for it and be willing and able to reciprocate in some way.

16

NETWORKING

Few of us succeed without the help of others. We all need someone else to provide a helping hand once in awhile. The previous chapter dealt with the concept of involving others in your business operation. The following material illustrates the application of these principles beyond your immediate circle of friends and acquaintances.

WHAT IS NETWORKING?

"Network" is among the most commonly used and misused buzz words today. A popular dictionary defines a network as "... *any net-like combination of things as in a network of vines or highways.*" From that basic definition the word has expanded and diversified its meaning. We now hear the word used in terms like *"computer network," "self-help support network," "professional network"* and *"personal network."* It is also common to hear the word used as a verb, as in *"networking"* or *"It is good to network,"* or as an adjective, as in *"network marketing"* or *"network meeting"* or *"network interview."*

Effective networking is essential to success in all businesses, large or small. The synergy of effective networking can be an energizing force, just as ineffective networking is a waste of time. Networking serves two very important functions. It can be a window on the world and an excellent promotional vehicle for you and your services. By gathering information about what is happening in businesses other than our own, we may benefit from the experience of others. We can import into our own business those practices that have contributed to the successes of others while avoiding their mistakes.

Windows can reflect back as well as let us see through them. Discussing our business practices with others can provide us with new views, much as a reflection in a window provides a different perspective on the room. A different perspective can generate new opportunities.

Chapter 13 outlined the use of networking as a marketing strategy. Network-facilitated third-party promotion is the most powerful form of word-of-mouth advertising. Having a credible third party promote our businesses will undoubtedly generate very exciting new business opportunities.

HOW NETWORKING WORKS

Like normal social conversation, networking opportunities can arise when two individuals happen to meet. If the two people don't know each other, they start looking for common areas of interest and may start exchanging information. At the end of the conversation each has learned something new from the other. There are three main ways of networking, each of which will be useful at different times.

Spontaneous Networking

Here, we interact with others under circumstances that do not have networking as a principal objective. Our meeting with the other person is totally by chance; we didn't plan to meet. We could be standing in line, meeting at a social event or even sitting beside each other on an airplane.

Apart from carrying business cards and an open mind, little preparation can be done for these chance encounters. During the conversation, common areas of interest are identified and useful information is exchanged. At the same time, subtle signals are exchanged, which influence what we do with the overt information. These signals enable us to evaluate the experience, credibility and personal style of our new acquaintances.

Keep the conversation brief. It is best to make arrangements to meet or talk later to continue your discussion. However, if neither of you has companions with you and there are no social restraints to your conversation, by all means go for it! Talk about your business and explore potential opportunities to your heart's delight. Ideally, at the end of the conversation each leaves with some follow-up plan in mind; it may be as simple as agreeing to get together "the next time I'm in town."

Planned Networking Opportunities
Because of the importance of networking, opportunities should not be left to chance. Indeed, individuals and organizations often create situations that enable like-minded people to get together. The range and nature of these networking events is limited only by the creativity of their organizers.

Large trade shows offer a heady brew of state-of-the-art technology, exhibitors, speakers and participants. Smaller groups meet regularly, often with a keynote speaker and an informal meal, to provide smaller and more focused networking sessions. Regardless of the size or format the purpose is the same — to enable people with similar interests to meet each other.

Having seen the potential of effective networking, many groups schedule events at regular intervals. As part of the process, ideas and business cards are exchanged and plans made for follow-up.

Unfortunately, the tendency with many of these groups is to develop an internal focus. If they are successful and enjoyable, the special network events become the end rather than the means. They may become mainly sociable gatherings of like-minded people, at which participants have little, if any, expectation of taking action on any business information they may gather.

One-on-one Meetings

These are probably the most effective form of networking. One individual initiates contact with another, with the stated expectation of exchanging information or ideas about a topic of mutual interest.

In practice, the relationship can develop as follows: Initial contact can be made by letter, by phone or personal contact and a mutually convenient meeting is arranged. The individual initiating the meeting should prepare for it by clarifying the information he wishes to gather. The non-initiating individual should give some consideration to the questions of "Who is this person?" and "What does he want from me?"

This form of networking can be very interesting and rewarding. It allows the participants to share control over the content, timing and format of their conversations. It does, however, require a high level of initiative, personal discipline and organization. A thank-you note or phone call from the initiator of the meeting to the other party will help ensure future co-operation.

NETWORKING IS A MEANS TO AN END; IT IS NOT AN END IN ITSELF

As a means to an end, networking is a strategy that we use to achieve personal or business goals. Similarly, when a business acquaintance tells me that she is unhappy with her electronic voice-mail system, she is using networking as a strategy for finding a solution to a problem. When I refer her to my very satisfactory answering service, she is on her own to pursue a solution to the problem.

In neither situation is the individual providing me with information in the belief that I might be interested in knowing it. Rather, they are doing it in the hope that I can give them information that will help them achieve their own goals.

NETWORKING IS AN EXCHANGE OF INFORMATION; IT IS NOT SELF-SERVING INFORMATION-GATHERING

In networking, as in every other part of life, we get back what we give out. Most of us have information and experience that would be useful to others. If we are prepared to pass on the benefit of our knowledge, we are likely to receive similar benefits in return. Conversely, if we seek only to gather information for our own use, our sources may soon dry up.

If, during our conversation about his social life, my friend also tells me about a new business opportunity, we are exchanging mutually beneficial information, we are helping each other. On the other hand, if my business acquaintance continues to use me as an unpaid information service, providing nothing in return, my willingness to provide information will decrease.

Obviously, it is prudent to be selective about the people and the occasions we select for networking purposes. Not everyone has information of interest to us, and, hard as it is to believe, there are people who have little interest in what we have to say. As well, there are many social, family, and other situations where business-related networking would be out of place.

NETWORKING IS FOCUSED AND DIRECTED; IT IS NOT RANDOM AND UNPLANNED

In today's world there is no shortage of information. In fact, most of us suffer from information overload. Since networking is a means to end, it is important to remain focused on that end. From a home business perspective, this end usually relates to improved operating efficiency or new business opportunities consistent with our business plans.

A well-focused information-gathering process should operate like a funnel with a built-in sieve. The funnel collects a broad flow of liquid and directs it into a narrower and more manageable stream. The same process occurs in networking when we collect a wide range of information from many sources and combine it mentally into more understandable information packages.

For example, the person seeking alternatives to electronic voice-mail could take the information provided by telephone answering and messaging services and combine it with what I and others have told her. Now she has a smaller, more understandable information package.

She may with the "mental" sieve strain out and discard extraneous information such as the technical specifications of the answering service equipment.

Bear in mind, however, that specific information that is not immediately useful may well turn out to be in the future. I continue to be amazed at how chance encounters often bear fruit in unexpected ways. These encounters with artists, sales representatives and others have often led me to very interesting and productive speaking engagements.

NETWORKING IS ONGOING; IT IS NOT INTERMITTENT

Information is dynamic — it is constantly changing. To ensure that your information base is kept current, make sure you continue networking. As well as helping to operate your business more successfully and serving your clients better, you will have more up-to-date information to share with others. Yesterday's news is of limited use.

Be warned, though, that "ongoing" does not mean "all the time and everywhere." We all need time away from business to enjoy friends and family. Most people would agree that social situations are inappropriate occasions to sell anything or recruit members for a marketing network. If you wish to pursue such discussions with someone whom you meet socially, you can exchange business cards and make an appointment to meet later.

17

JUST DOING IT

As you develop and build your home business you are more likely to be successful if you follow these ten commandments and avoid the deadly sins.

THE TEN COMMANDMENTS OF RUNNING YOUR HOME BUSINESS

1. Maintain steady business hours.

Although you are physically separated from the business community, your home business operation must be accessible to and compatible with it. This means operating your business during hours compatible with those of your existing and potential customers, contacts and referral sources.

Further, by maintaining steady business hours, you will develop the discipline of concentrating on your work responsibilities and minimizing potential impact from household distractions. Equally important, you will minimize the spillover of business activities into family and social life.

2.   Maintain a separate business telephone line.

A separate business telephone line will make it easier for clients to contact you. The line may be listed in the telephone directory and Yellow Pages if you choose. With a separate line, all business calls will be handled in a professional manner.

A separate line will also make it possible to close shop when you are no longer working. An answering machine or answering service will ensure that business calls are answered appropriately after normal business hours.

3.   Establish your office away from living areas.

As much as possible, your business activities should be separated from your personal activities. This will ensure that client paperwork does not get used for grocery lists or other family notes and messages. The physical separation will also help protect the confidentiality of your dealings with clients.

Having your office away from living areas will also help you maintain the personal discipline that you need to work at home. Some people go so far as to physically leave the house when it is time to go to work. They may walk around the block, re-enter the house (often by a different door) and proceed to the office.

4.   Organize your office efficiently.

Unless your office is located in a very unusual setting, you can expect few clients to visit. (One consultant, who for a short time operated his business from his sailboat moored in a local marina reports that while there, every one of his clients came to see him!) As a result of not having to maintain appearances for clients, there is a risk of your home

office becoming an unmanageable jumble of paper, books
and so on.

You should organize and maintain your home office
according to the same standards that you would use in regular office premises. As well as helping to reinforce your
personal discipline, efficient organization will prevent
important pieces of paper from going astray.

5.   Establish and follow definite work routines.
Your home office work routines should not be significantly
different from those you followed in other work situations.
This will involve planning your day and working according
to that plan.

6.   Use fixed price contracts.
Prices for your services should be a set contract based on
the value that your clients will receive; i.e., a set fee rather
than an hourly or daily rate.

7.   Sell value.
Clients are primarily interested in what they will be receiving for their money; they are less interested in either the
time you spend on a project or your rates. Paying for your
services on a fixed price basis, clients can attach a cost to the
benefits that they will receive.

8.   Follow your business plan and your marketing plan.
Once completed, these plans represent a significant investment of time and energy. They are not intended to be historical documents cast in stone and bound for the archives.
They should serve as road maps or blueprints, providing
you with an overall sense of direction. Your plans should
give you the inspiration and direction to keep forging ahead

to your goals when you seem to be bogged down in details.

For future reference, you should record any changes or modifications to your business or marketing plan. This will help ensure the accuracy of your planning process the next time you go through it. It will also help ensure that your goals and strategies are realistic in light of your services and your clients.

9. Extend your services through sub-contracts, joint ventures and part-time staff.

With finite resources, there are limits to the services that you can provide directly and limits to the number and type of clients whom you can serve. By sub-contracting services to others, or working on projects as a joint venture, you can dramatically increase your service potential.

Similarly, by hiring part-time support staff, you may also significantly increase your service capability. The same principles apply: know what you need and ask for it.

10. Stand behind your services.

Your services are at least as good as those of your competitors. If this were not true, you should not have started your business in the first place. Your commitment to providing top-quality services should be high enough that you can guarantee your clients' satisfaction. This is not "satisfaction guaranteed or money refunded." The guarantee is "satisfaction guaranteed or I'll do whatever it takes to make you happy." Note also that you are guaranteeing your services, not the end results. You can guarantee your services because you can control them; you can't guarantee end results because you cannot control your clients' actions. Ensure that you and your customer understand the distinction.

THE SEVEN DEADLY SINS OF RUNNING
YOUR HOME BUSINESS

1. Allowing personal interruptions during business hours.
There is no perfect working environment. In traditional
office settings, interruptions come in the form of telephone
calls, unscheduled visitors, co-workers and supervisors
shifting your priorities and support staff seeking direction
and instructions.

The potential for interruptions is equally high in the
home office. On your residence telephone line, you may be
subjected to unsolicited telemarketing and sundry personal
or family-related calls. Neighbors may drop by for a chat;
family members might leave you with a list of chores and
errands. The list of potential interruptions goes on.

To minimize these interruptions, you can stop answering the residence telephone, or at least use an answering
machine during your working hours.

Remind everyone, including yourself, that you are
home to work, not to perform chores and errands for yourself or others.

2. Allowing yourself to be distracted.
Frequently, when people find out that I work at home they
tell me how they couldn't do it because they would be distracted by the fridge, the TV, the VCR, the bed, the swim-
ming pool, the garden or whatever. I have found that as
long as I do not allow myself to think about all the possible
distractions they simply do not exist for me.

Apart from firming up your personal discipline, there
are no guaranteed techniques to prevent you from becom-

ing distracted. You might try rewarding yourself with a trip to the fridge or a nap only after you have achieved specific work objectives. You might also try going for a walk or performing some exercises if you feel overcome by distractions.

You might also schedule some work-related activities away from your home office at regular intervals. This should give you the break that you need and provide for increased concentration.

3.   Working on one project at a time.

You are likely to be more easily distracted if you work on only one project at a time. With a number of projects active at any given time, you can minimize distractions by moving from one to another. Make sure you have one project at an appropriate break point before you move on the next. Otherwise you will waste too much time trying to remember where you were and what you had planned to do next.

4.   Allowing yourself to be seduced into working all the time.

For workaholics, home offices are deadly traps. It is simply too easy to slip into the office for a few minutes — or hours — after dinner or before going to bed. For those individuals who work to escape or to hide from other responsibilities, a home office is too convenient a hiding place.

Unless absolutely necessary, do not go back to your office after normal business hours. If you have a small piece of work to finish, or are facing a major deadline, by all means put in the extra time. Work late, start early or do whatever you would normally do in a traditional office setting. Once the project is finished, take lieu time instead of over-time and get away from the office. Do not get into the practice of going into the office after business hours just because it is convenient to do so.

5.   Discounting your rates.

Good clients, i.e., those who bring in repeat business and who pay their bills, expect quality service over low prices. By discounting your rates, you are giving your clients the message that the value of your services is lower because you work at home. You don't believe this; why should you give this message to your clients?

By following commandments 6 and 7, you can present your fees in such a manner that your clients may believe they are receiving lower fees because of your lower overhead. Let your clients draw their own conclusions; under no circumstances should you encourage them to believe that your services are worth less because you work at home.

6.   Marketing sporadically.

Although a risk for all businesses, sporadic marketing is especially perilous for home businesses. Being physically removed from the business mainstream, it is often difficult to get out of the house to maintain contact with current and potential clients. Marketing is probably easier if you can actually see members of your target market on a regular basis. As outlined earlier, marketing is an ongoing activity. You must practise it on a frequent basis. To do otherwise is to risk isolation from your market. Once isolated, you will have to work twice as had to establish your position amongst your competitors.

7.   Working so much for your clients that you do not work on your own business.

In its extreme form, this is the case of the cobbler's children who didn't have any shoes. The key to running any successful business — outside the home or home-based — is to give top priority to clients. It is also important to remember that your own business is a client. It has needs and expectations that must be met to survive. Providing the fastest and the best client service means little if your own business is falling in on itself.

18

MORE RESOURCES

This book began with an entrepreneurial assessment. As a result of this assessment, you have either skimmed through the book and decided that running your own business is not what you want to do or have reviewed the material and are now ready to proceed with the development of your business. In either case, you will no doubt require further assistance as you proceed. The following material is intended to assist with this journey.

USEFUL BOOKS

The books included are listed as a sampling of those that I have found useful to some degree or other.

This list is by no means complete. Because of the vagaries of book distribution, it is very likely that there are some excellent books available of which I am unaware. If so, please let me know; I will try to locate the books that you suggest, and if appropriate include them in future editions. Conversely, your favorite bookseller or library may be unable to locate some of the books published by smaller and less-known publishers. To address this possible problem I have included specific addresses where appropriate.

Job Search

If you have no interest in starting a home business, you will most likely be continuing your job search. Bookstores and libraries are well stocked with excellent material and new works come onto the market regularly. The following titles represent some of the best books to add to your resource bank.

The 1995 What Colour Is Your Parachute? A Practical Manual for Job-Hunters and Career Changers by Richard Bolles.

Updated annually since 1975, this is the definitive work of job search and career development. Whether you are simply looking for a new job or are unsure of what to do with the rest of your life, this book is a must-have. It is published by Ten Speed Press, P.O. Box 7123, Berkeley, California 94707. Also highly recommended are the companion works *The Three Boxes of Life and How to Get Out Of Them* and *Where Do I Go From Here With My Life?* by the same author.

From Fired to Hired: The Middle Manager's Guide to Job Searching in the 90s by Reg Pirie.

Published in mid-1994, this book was written and published by someone who has actually moved from being fired to being hired. Now an outplacement counselor, the author provides new and unique insights into today's job market. The book contains excellent material on the four key elements of job search: focus, organization, research and activity. Published by Ink Ink Publishing, the book is available in the U.S. and Canada through the distributor, Christie and Christie by phoning 1-800-263-1991.

Selecting a Home Business

If you have decided that you would like to operate your own home business but do not know which one would be best, any of the following books will offer suggestions. U.S. readers might benefit from the Canadian book listed; Canadian readers will definitely benefit from the U.S. books listed.

> *Bright Business Ideas — Innovative and Inventive Ideas That Can Become a Golden Opportunity* by Brian Lovig.
>
> The author, who is also an entrepreneur, draws on his experience in sales and marketing to offer dozens of concepts that are easy, and in many cases fun, to develop and implement. Published by Bright Publishing Inc., the book is available from the publisher in both Canada and the U.S. Addresses are Bright Publishing Inc., Box 24002, Downtown P.O., Kelowna, B.C., Canada V1Y 9P9 and Bright Publishing Inc., Room 261, Box 5000, Oroville, Washington, U.S.A. 98844.

> *Entrepreneur Magazine's 184 Businesses Anyone Can Start and Make a Lot of Money* by the editors of *Entrepreneur*.
>
> This detailed work contains start-up costs and profit profiles for a broad range of businesses ranging from Athletic Shoe Sales to Vocational Training Services. Published by

Bantam, Books, 1st edition 1981, 2nd edition 1990.

The Best Home-Based Francishes by Gregory Matusky and The Philip Lief Group.

This comprehensive work presents an excellent introduction to the world of franchising and then offers profiles on almost 100 franchises that can be operated from home. Published by Doubleday, 1992.

101 Best Businesses to Start by Charon Kahn and The Philip Lief Group.

Another catalogue of business ideas with guidelines for start-up and operating costs, profit projections, and staffing needs, this book includes case studies that present both the pitfalls and rewards of starting a business. The book was published by Doubleday in 1992.

Creating the Home Business You Want

Not all home businesses are adaptations of ideas developed by others. In fact, the most successful are often created by individuals to meet their own needs. The following may help you create the business you want.

The Path of Least Resistance by Robert Fritz.

This book teaches how to create what you want. When combined with sound business practices, this easy-to-use resource will enable the reader to create his or her own unique and personal business. Published by Ballantine Books, 1989.

Making A Living Without A Job by Barbara J. Winter.

Being without a job does not mean not working. It can mean working for yourself. The author shows how you can go about this. She even offers suggestions as to suitable business opportunities. Published by Bantam in 1993.

Creativity in Business by Michael Ray and Rochelle Myers.

The title says it all; this book is all about applying the principles of creativity in developing and managing businesses. Published by Doubleday, 1989.

General Management and Marketing

There is no shortage of titles on this topic. The following books are worthy of note. As well as these, you might also scout out a good book on bookkeeping, record-keeping and accounting. At the very least you should know enough about these topics to understand what your statements mean.

What They Don't Teach You At Harvard Business School by Mark H. McCormack, 1984.

Carrying the subtitle Notes From A Street-Smart Executive, this book is in effect a practical course on dealing with people, sales and negotiation and running a business.

Also recommended, giving more tips and suggestions on selling, communicating and entrepreneuring is *What They Still Don't Teach You at*

Harvard Business School, 1989, by the same author. Both books published by Bantam.

Guerrilla Marketing: Secrets For Making Big Profits from Your Small Business, 1984, by Jay Conrad Levinson.

This is an excellent beginner's guide to marketing. It provides many innovative cost-effective suggestions for small business marketing activities. Its companion volume *Guerrilla Advertising*, 1989, is also highly recommended. Both books published by Houghton Mifflin Company.

PERIODICALS

Just as the growth of home businesses is giving rise to new books, it is generating a wealth of new magazines, newsletters and other periodicals. The lifespan of these periodicals varies. Some cease publication after a few issues while others thrive and mature. Because of the long lead time involved in preparing a book such as this, it is virtually impossible to include a list of periodicals that is still accurate when the book is published. Accordingly, no specific periodicals have been listed.

This does not mean that the periodicals that are available are not good. Start your search by asking for home business magazines where you buy other periodicals. I assure you the will be plenty from which to choose. Public libraries, college and university libraries offer many periodicals as well as periodical indices to help you research specific topics. And, of course, librarians can be extremely helpful.

ASSOCIATIONS

Home business associations and networks are also spring-
ing up like mushrooms after a rain and often disappear just
as quickly. Ask around and you will be able to find a home
business group of some kind in your local municipality. If
none exists, start one. Bear in mind that participating in
associations and organizations is a means to an end and not
an end in itself. Before committing yourself to active participation in any organization, review the comments about
organizations, found in Chapters 13 (Marketing) and 16
(Networking).

 If you would like to join business organizations and be
on mailing lists, the following information may be a good
starting point for you. Through the contacts that you make
in these organizations, you will learn of many other groups
that you can join, increasing your opportunities to extend
your network of personal contacts.

 There are thousands of organizations that provide some
level of assistance to potential and new operators of home
businesses. These organizations can be classified as local
business associations, trade associations or franchise associations.

1. Local Business Associations

Local associations not only provide excellent networking
opportunities, but offer direct and immediate services, such
as discounts on purchases and training workshops.
Established to serve local interests, these organizations are
seldom listed in national directories. Locating local cham-
bers of commerce and boards of trade is usually fairly simple; you'll need a telephone book, and perhaps a visit to
your local reference library. Locating specific local business

organizations can be a more difficult task, and it's a good opportunity to try out the networking techniques discussed in Chapter 16. As well, on-line bulletin boards can be excellent sources of information about business associations and their activities.

I have encountered a number of local business groups as a result of networking. One such group is EntreNET Brampton, a very active group based in Brampton, Ontario. Self-described as " ... an association of small business entrepreneurs working together and helping each other grow successful businesses ... ," EntreNET Brampton's membership services include monthly networking meetings and theme workshops.

EntreNET Brampton
3946 Steeles Avenue East
Brampton, Ontario L6T 3Y7
Phone: 905-790-6255

The founder of this organization is willing to assist with the development of similar organizations in other areas.

Canadian Association of Home Business
1200 East Prince of Wales Drive
Ottawa, Ontario K2C 1M9
Phone: 613-723-7233

Although based in Eastern Ontario, this group has indicated a desire to work with home business operators in other areas to assist with the development of local chapters.

2. Trade Associations
These associations often provide useful start-up information and management and marketing advice to new business

operations. Space prohibits a complete listing of all potentially useful trade associations. Therefore, I will use two
examples of new businesses to demonstrate how to locate
the appropriate trade association for your new business.

In the first example, a prospective desktop publisher is
looking for a trade association that might offer her some
start-up assistance. At the local library, she searches the key
word index of the *Encyclopedia of Associations* for reference to
desktop publishing organizations. Here she finds the
National Association of DeskTop Publishers listed as entry
number 6083, located in volume 1, part 2, page 765. The entry
provides the address (462 Old Boston Street, Topsfield, MA
01983), phone numbers (phone: 508-887-7900; fax; 508-887-
6117 and toll free: 800-874-4113), and information about the
association's services to members, including general information, purchasing discounts and various support services.

The second example is that of a craftsperson in the inte-
rior of British Columbia, looking for a provincial or regional craft association. His search would also begin at the public library, this time using the *Directory of Associations in
Canada*. Searching the key word index for "British
Columbia", he finds the Craft Association of British
Columbia listed as entry 02268, found on page 294 of the
same book. As above, the entry includes address (1386
Cartwright Street, Granville Island, B.C., V6H 3R8), phone
numbers (phone: 604-687-7270; fax: 604-687-6511), and
information about the organization. Included in this listing
are dates of conferences for craftspeople.

You can use the same procedure to identify appropriate
trade associations for your business. Of the thousands of
organizations listed in the multivolume encyclopedia set
and the directory, there is undoubtedly at least one that can

help. While in the public library, you might also have a look at the home business books, usually numbered 658.041 according to the library cataloging system.

3.   Franchise Associations

These associations provide invaluable information and assistance to potential franchisees. Either the International Franchise Association or the Canadian Franchise Association are important first contacts in your investigation of specific franchises. For example, the Canadian Franchise Association offers an information kit designed to assist you with the evaluation process.

Canadian Franchise Association
Suite 201, Building 12
5045 Orbiter Drive
Mississauga, Ontario L4W 4Y4
Phone: 905-625-2896
Fax: 905-635-9076

International Franchise Association
1350 New York Avenue N.W, Suite 900
Washington D.C. 20005
Phone: 202-628-8000
Fax: 202-628-0812
Fax on Demand: 202-628-3432
Prodigy (on line computer connection): RXNS906

Before committing yourself to participation in any organization, know what services are being offered. Whether you expect to receive personal development services, such as training, or business development opportunities, such as leads and referrals, ensure that the organization can *and does* deliver what you expect.

GOVERNMENT ASSISTANCE

Assuming normal distribution of this book in Canada and the U.S., more than 65 federal, state, provincial and territorial governments have jurisdiction over and offer assistance to small business in general and home business in particular. Several thousand municipal governments also influence home business operations.

The good news here is that there is a wide range of assistance available to all kinds of small businesses. The bad news is that the assistance is often difficult to locate. The best place to start is with the person who looks after promoting economic development on behalf of your municipal government. The next best place is your local library. Ask the librarian for information about government assistance to home businesses.

Following-up on any of the resources previously listed is something like opening Pandora's box. You have no idea what is going to come from your efforts. Most of the books, like this one, will contain further references to other publications. Try not to be seduced into going after all the books and resources listed. Remember that you are looking at the various resources as a possible source of help. You are not undertaking an exhaustive research project.

19

NOW YOU
TELL ME...

ABOUT YOUR HOME BUSINESS

If you currently operate a home business, I would like to know how you are doing. Tell me what has made your business successful so I can incorporate these factors into my own operation and advise others.

Just because we learn from our mistakes, we don't all have to make the same ones. What would you advise home business people to avoid?

Please take a few minutes and describe your home business using the following guidelines. Mail your response to the address listed below.

- What product or service do you provide?
- To whom do you provide this product or service?
- What secrets of success would you give to someone starting his or her own home business?
- What pitfalls or traps should be avoided? How?
- If you had to start your business all over again, what would you do differently?

To assist all home business people, I plan to gather this information and publish it in a future edition. I will use actual case examples, with the prior approval of the people involved. If I use your business as an example, I will send you a complementary copy of the publication in which your business is featured. To make this possible, please include your name and address with your responses.

Mail your response to:

Larry Easto
c/o Doubleday Canada Limited
105 Bond Street
Toronto, Ontario
M5B 1Y3
Canada

ABOUT THE BOOK

As discussed in Chapter 14, client feedback is vital to the success of a business venture. This is true of all business ventures, including the writing and publication of this book.

Subject to readers' interest, I anticipate publishing subsequent editions. I would like you to tell me how I can improve future editions and how I can make them more helpful for people like you.

Please complete the following brief semi-formal evaluation and mail it to me.

I appreciate your co-operation.

Larry Easto

1. What did you like best about the book?

2. What content should be added to make the book more relevant to you and your situation?

3. What content should be changed to make the book more relevant to you and your situation?

4. How can the inside design and layout be improved?

5. What general comments and observations do you have?

NOTES

1. Naisbitt, John, *Global Paradox* (New York: Avon Books, 1994)
2. Rowan, Roy, *The Intuitive Manager* (New York: Berkley Books, 1986)
3. Matusky, Gregory, *The Best Home Based Franchises* (New York: Doubleday, 1992)
4. Popcorn, Faith, *The Popcorn Report* (New York: Doubleday, 1991)
5. Sakaiya, Tachi, *The Knowledge Value Revolution or A History of the Future* (New York: Kodansha America Inc., 1991)
6. Popcorn
7. Popcorn
8. Popcorn
9. Popcorn
10. Sakaiya
11. Sakaiya
12. Huge, Ernest C., *Total Quality: An Executive's Guide for the 1990s* (Homewood, Ill: Dow Jones Irwin, 1990)
13. Drucker, Peter F., *Management Tasks: Responsibilities Practices* (New York: Harper & Row, 1973)

INDEX